From the
Classroom
To the
Workplace

Volume I

Grocery

Retail

Housekeeping

Juanita Pritchard & Karla Stone

S0-AZS-208

About the Authors

Juanita Pritchard is a Vocational Evaluator and Assistive Technology Specialist for the Cobb County School System in Marietta, Georgia. She received her Ed.S in Intellectual Disabilities from Valdosta State College. She has spent ten years in the classroom and nine years as a community-based vocational trainer with moderately and severely intellectually disabled high school students.

Karla Stone is a Community-Based Instructional Liaison for the Cobb County School System in Marietta, Georgia. She has a Master's Degree in Special Education with an emphasis on moderate and severe intellectual disabilities from Georgia State University. She had 11 years of classroom experience with a wide range of special needs students prior to doing hands-on community-based vocational training for four years.

Acknowledgments

We would like to acknowledge Sandra McKibben for the inspiration she has provided us not only with her artwork in this book but her devotion and commitment to special needs students for 25 years. We would also like to express our appreciation to the Cobb County Community-Based Instruction staff who have supported us throughout this endeavor.

Dedication

This book is dedicated to those people who believed we could do this even when we weren't so sure, with a special thanks to our families:
David, Rachel, Brian, and Nicholas
Jeff, Sarah, and Amanda
for supporting us in completing this book.

© Copyright 1997 by the Mayer-Johnson Co. All rights reserved. The activities within this manual may be reproduced for classroom or educational purposes. This work may not be reproduced or copied in its entirety in any form or by any means graphic, electronic, or mechanical, including photocopying, recording, taping, or information and retrieval, without the written permission of the publisher.

Mayer-Johnson Co.
P.O. Box 1579
Solana Beach, CA 92075-7579
Phone (619) 550-0084
Fax (619) 550-0449

Second Printing, August 1999

Printed in the U.S.A.

ISBN 1-884135-34-X

Table of Contents

Introduction

Overview

As special educators, we are given the task of preparing our students for a world that is often challenging to access and difficult to understand. One way to ease this task is to make available as many opportunities as possible to accustom them to situations they may face as adults. We believe that the most important teaching is that which prepares our students to become proficient at skills at each individual's maximum level of independence. We hope that in these pages will be found some of the tools that will make this possible for the classroom teachers. These chapters contain outlines and activities that will interpret vocational realities so that they may be used in the classroom. Please note that this is the first book in a series of two. The second book, *From the Classroom to the Workplace, Volume II,* address vocational skills in the areas of Office/clerical and Restaurant/food service using the same format.

Target Population

The target population for the book is broad. It is meant to embrace students who are middle and high school aged who receive services for intellectual disabilities, orthopedic impairments, emotional/behavioral disorders, speech and language impairments, traumatic brain injury, autism, pervasive developmental delays as well as nonreaders and low academic achievers. Augmentative communication device overlays are included in each chapter to maximize interactive communication. Hands-on experiences, reinforcement pages on several different levels, and suggested community outings with follow-up worksheets all combine to make this a versatile resource for special educators who want to offer their students a more realistic approach to learning vocational skills.

How to use this book

The three chapters in this book will provide educators with information to improve students' vocational skills in the areas of

- Grocery
- Retail
- Housekeeping/Laundry

Each chapter includes suggestions for hands-on activities designed to teach skills actually used in each specific vocational area. Students will enjoy the practical application of these skills, and teachers and students alike will enjoy the accompanying worksheets that reinforce vocabulary, work habits, and critical discrimination skills.

Communication Overlays

Communication overlays are included to allow students with augmentative devices to participate to the fullest extent of their ability. School-to-home communication is encouraged by the parent letter and suggested task calendar provided with each section. Community-experience components are included in each chapter to give teachers suggestions on appropriate activities for generalization of vocational skills in actual community settings.

Worksheets

Each objective has two or more worksheets to use for generalization and reinforcement of skills. The worksheets were designed so that a wide variety of learning styles and abilities levels could be accommodated. Both readers and nonreaders can benefit from the activities. Whenever possible, the symbols used for overlays are also used within the worksheets to allow extra practice. Any time a worksheet uses symbols, it provides the teacher with more options for participation:

- Students can work independently without reading.
- Students can write or cut and paste.
- Symbols can be cut out and used for other activities.
- Students with physical limitations can use the symbols instead of a writing activity.

Every effort was made to keep symbols consistent. No student should be denied participation in any of the activities suggested.

General Skills Used in the Work Force

Very few job sites use skills in isolation. Most skills that are necessary in any one work cluster will generalize to other work clusters. This makes teaching the skills in the classroom as well as in the community essential. On the following page is a chart of the basic work/job skills used by the six major job clusters:

- Retail
- Grocery Store
- Laundry/Housekeeping
- Food Service/Restaurant
- Clerical/Office worker
- Horticulture

General Skills Used in Work Force

Legend: Often = Used Often (shaded) · Occ. = Used occasionally (zigzag)

Skill	Retail	Grocery Store	Laundry/ Housekeeping	Food Service	Clerical	Horticulture
Facing Shelves	Often	Often	Occ.	Often	Occ.	Occ.
Categorizing food/nonfood	Occ.	Often		Often		
Packaging/Unpacking	Often	Often	Occ.	Often	Occ.	Occ.
Moving/Stacking boxes safely	Often	Often	Occ.	Often	Occ.	
Folding	Often	Occ.	Often	Occ.	Occ.	
Hanging clothes	Often		Occ.	Occ.		
Counting items	Often	Often	Often	Often	Often	Often
Match to sample	Often	Often	Often	Often	Often	Often
Trash disposal	Often	Often	Often	Often	Often	Often
Sort: "clean/dirty" • by color	Often	Often	Often	Often	Often	Often
• by size • by number • by style	Often	Often	Often	Often	Often	Often
Identify and use cleaning materials	Often	Often	Often	Often	Occ.	Often
Make bed			Often			
Vacuum	Often	Occ.	Often	Often		
Sweep/mop	Often	Often	Often	Often	Often	Often
Replace items in correct order	Often	Often	Often	Often	Often	Often
General systematic cleaning	Often	Often	Often	Often	Often	Often
Load cart with specific items	Often	Often	Often	Occ.	Occ.	
Basic food preparation		Occ.		Often		
Dishwashing	Occ.	Occ.	Occ.	Often		
Sorting and rolling silverware				Often		
Condiments: filling, cleaning storing				Often		
Pricing	Often	Often			Occ.	
Using Labels	Often	Often	Occ.	Occ.	Often	
Matching stock #s	Often	Often	Occ.	Occ.	Often	
Filing/Sorting papers	Occ.	Occ.	Occ.	Occ.	Often	Occ.

Legend:  = Used Often   ∿∿∿∿ = Used occassionally

General Work Overlay

Guidelines for Generalization of Classroom Activities

I. Make It Real
   A. Use real items and use them in an appropriate context.
   B. Work in a variety of settings:
      standing, alone, in a crowd, where it's quiet or noisy.
   C. Make it varied.
   D. Make it worth their time (not "baby" stuff).

II. Make Students Independent
   A. Expect students to set up their own workspace.
   B. Set up sign-in and sign-out situations.
   C. Expect students to verbalize/communicate their needs without prompting.
   D. Make the work area accessible and set up for maximum independence.
   E. Expect students to follow instructions to a conclusion.

III. Make Students Work For It
   A. Have enough work for a minimum of 45 minutes, up to 4 hours.
   B. Show your respect to students by providing challenging tasks.
   C. Plan "chaos" to provide experience in situations that don't follow the normal routine.
   D. Increase stamina and endurance to 2 hours of work without a break, standing if possible.

IV. Make Work Their Future
   A. Set up expectations for work at home, at school, and after graduation.
   B. Tell them why skills are important.
   C. If it doesn't directly relate to their life after high school - *Don't waste their time (and yours)*.

V. Points To Ponder
   A. <u>Practice!</u> <u>Practice!</u> <u>Practice!</u>
   B. Emphasize manners, grooming, and eye contact at all times.
   C. <u>Never</u> say a student can't do (or learn) a task. Assume that everyone will be successful. Your job is to find the missing piece(s) that will make it possible.
   D. <u>Always</u> use adaptive communication devices - <u>Always!</u> You wouldn't forget to use a wheelchair or hearing aid.
   E. Partial participation is as important as independent success.
   F. If you can't explain how what you are teaching relates to a job or to essential daily living needs, you shouldn't be teaching it. (i.e. maps of foreign countries when the student doesn't know where he lives, rote math facts when the student can't identify and/or count out money).
   G. Use the computer for more than "games" and "practice." It is an integral part of our modern life: stores, libraries, most jobs.
   H. Have students request job applications from a variety of businesses. Help them make a job application resource notebook.

Grocery Store Unit

Grocery Store Unit

Vocational opportunities in a grocery store are important possibilities for learners with special needs. In this unit, students are introduced to courtesy clerk skills. These include:

- Categorizing items
- Correct bagging procedures
- Returning items to the correct aisle
- Facing shelves

Support materials for this unit include a variety of communication overlays specific to these tasks, worksheets on several levels, folder games, data collection and assessment forms, as well as a listing of vocabulary words and related concepts. Also included are forms designed to foster communication between school and home. Objectives for this unit include:

Objective 1: *Categorizing groceries (page 15)*.
Objective 2: *"Face" (straighten) shelves (page 25)*.
Objective 3: *Bagging groceries (page 31)*.
Objective 4: *Customer interaction (page 39)*.
Objective 5: *Personal appearance (page 61)*.

There are standard forms and overlays that are used for each objective. These include:

Vocational Update Letter to Parents — Use this form to send home with the student before the unit objective begins. It will give the parent or caregiver an overview of the unit objective plus extend the activity into the home (see page 4).

Calendar of Skills — Home activities that help reinforce skills learned in school (see page 5).

Vocabulary List — Common vocabulary words used throughout the five objectives (see page 6).

Evaluation/Documentation Forms — Use these forms to assess goal achievement and/or formulate IEP goals and objectives (see pages 7-10).

Same/Different Overlay — Simple overlay used with many of the unit objectives (see page 11).

Same/Different and Yes/No Overlay — A four-choice overlay used with many of the unit objectives (see page 12).

Yes/No Overlay - A two-choice overlay used with several of the unit objectives (see page 13).

Vocational Update

Dear Parents,

In class, we are working on a unit to learn skills important to working in a grocery store.

These are some vocabulary words we are using:

These are some activities you might want to try at home:

Thank you for your support in this important learning experience. Please sign and return.

Very truly yours,

_____

Parent signature _____

Calendar of Skills

☐ Let your child put away groceries at home.	☐ Have your child bag groceries at the store.

☐ At home, let your child show you 5 cold items and 5 not cold items.

☐ At the grocery store, let your child find items by matching them to coupon pictures.

☐ At the grocery store, let your child return an item you have taken from the shelf.

☐ At dinner, discuss which foods would be "squishy" or fragile (eggs, bread, etc.).

☐ Look through a magazine with your child. Identify pictures of "food" and "non-food" items.

☐ Play a "visualization" game. Name a grocery store item and have your child tell where to find it.

☐ Stack cans from your kitchen. Stores usually stack 2 high and 2 deep.

☐ Play a word game. Name pairs of items and ask if they go in a bag together (nuts/shampoo, meat/butter).

Parents,

Above is a suggested calendar of skills for our unit on Grocery Store skills. Please try to do seven out of ten of these activities with your child to enrich our work at school. Initial the skills you are able to complete and return the list by_____ : Students who return the calendar with seven of ten items initialed will receive _____ .

Thank you for your support,

_____

Vocabulary Words - Grocery Store Unit

manager	customer	cold
eye contact	tip	wet
plastic	paper	bag groceries
soft	cart	soap
food	nonfood	smile
not cold	dry	cashier
bottom	cans	top
price	facing	shelf
bottle	glass	load
not soft	heavy	light

Evaluation/Documentation

The evaluation and documentation instruments are included to help the teacher track the skills each student has attempted. They can be helpful when assessing goal achievement and formulating IEP goals and objectives. There are two different forms. The teacher may choose to use one or the other or both, depending on the needs of the class.

Grocery Store
IEP Goals and Objectives

The student will. . .

- ☐ Demonstrate categories necessary to correctly bag groceries:
    - ☐ food/nonfood
    - ☐ cold/not cold
    - ☐ wet/dry
    - ☐ soft ("squishable")

- ☐ Demonstrate necessary skills to "face" (or straighten) shelves.

- ☐ Demonstrate proper procedure for grocery bagging and transferring bagged items effectively (counter to cart to car).

- ☐ Demonstrate awareness of the following appropriate interaction behaviors with customers:
    - ☐ eye contact
    - ☐ smiling
    - ☐ responding/acquiring information
        - ☐ paper or plastic?
        - ☐ do you need help?
        - ☐ where is your car?
        - ☐ where do you want your groceries?
    - ☐ social amenities
        - ☐ please
        - ☐ thank you
        - ☐ have a nice day

- ☐ Demonstrate an understanding of the importance of personal appearance in the workplace:
    - ☐ uniforms/appropriate clothes
    - ☐ grooming
    - ☐ appropriate accessories (jewelry, hats, bandanas, etc.)

Evaluation Documentation: Grocery Store Unit
Individual Student Format

Student's Name _____ Objectives	worksheet	worksheet	worksheet	practice	worksheet	activity	activity	community	overlay	overlay		
1. Categories necessary to bag groceries												
Food/nonfood												
Cold/not cold												
Wet/dry												
Soft												
2. Necessary skills to "face" (straighten) shelves												
3. Proper procedure for grocery bagging & transferring bagged items (counter/cart/car)												
4. Appropriate interaction behaviors:												
Eye contact												
Smiling												
Responding to customer												
Requesting/acquiring information												
Paper or plastic?												
Do you need help?												
Where is your car?												
Where do you want your groceries?												
Social amenities												
Please, thank you, have a nice day!												
5. Importance of personal appearance in workplace												
Uniforms, appropriate clothes												
Grooming												
Appropriate accessories (jewelry, hats, etc.)												

Evaluation Documentation: Grocery Store Unit
Total Class Format

Objectives	students																
1. Categories necessary to bag groceries:																	
Food/nonfood																	
Cold/not cold																	
Wet/dry																	
Soft																	
2. Necessary skills to "face" (straighten) shelves																	
3. Proper procedure for grocery bagging & transferring bagged items (counter/car/car)																	
4. Appropriate interaction behaviors:																	
Eye contact																	
Smiling																	
Responding to customer																	
Requesting/acquiring information																	
Paper or plastic?																	
Do you need help?																	
Where is your car?																	
Where do you want your groceries?																	
Social amenities																	
Please, thank you, have a nice day!																	
5. Importance of personal appearance in workplace																	
Uniforms, appropriate clothes																	
Grooming																	
Appropriate accessories (jewelry, hats, etc.)																	

Same/Different Overlay

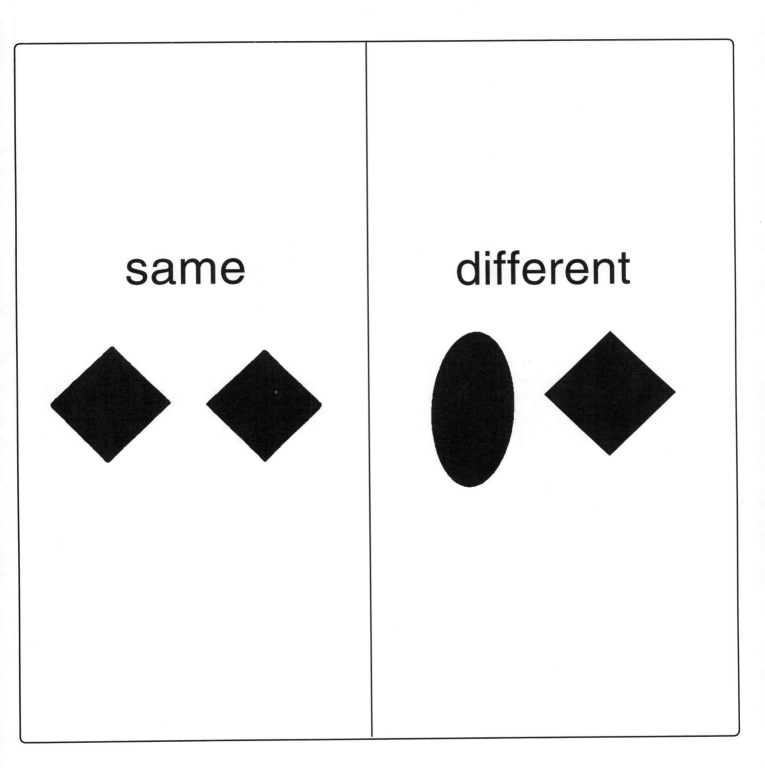

same

different

Same/Different and
Yes/No Overlay

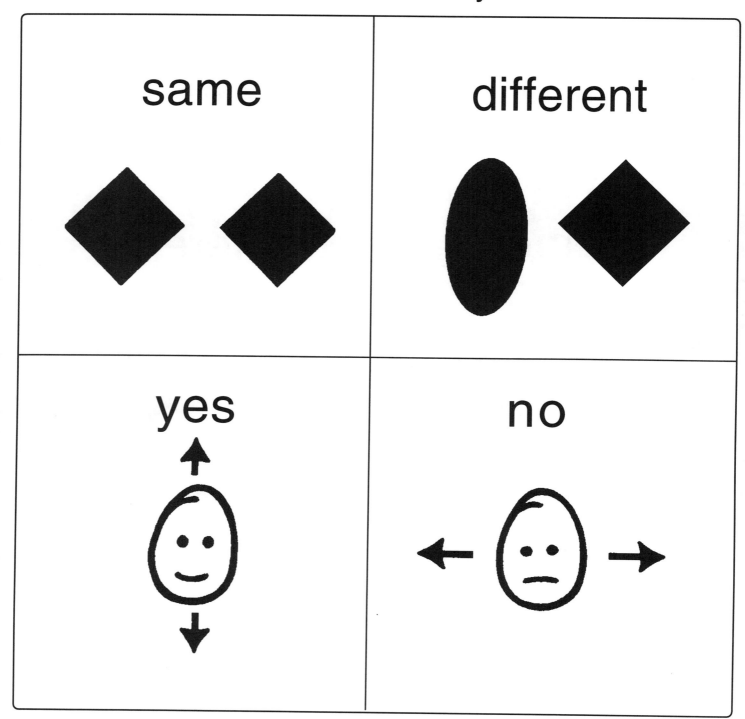

Yes/No Overlay

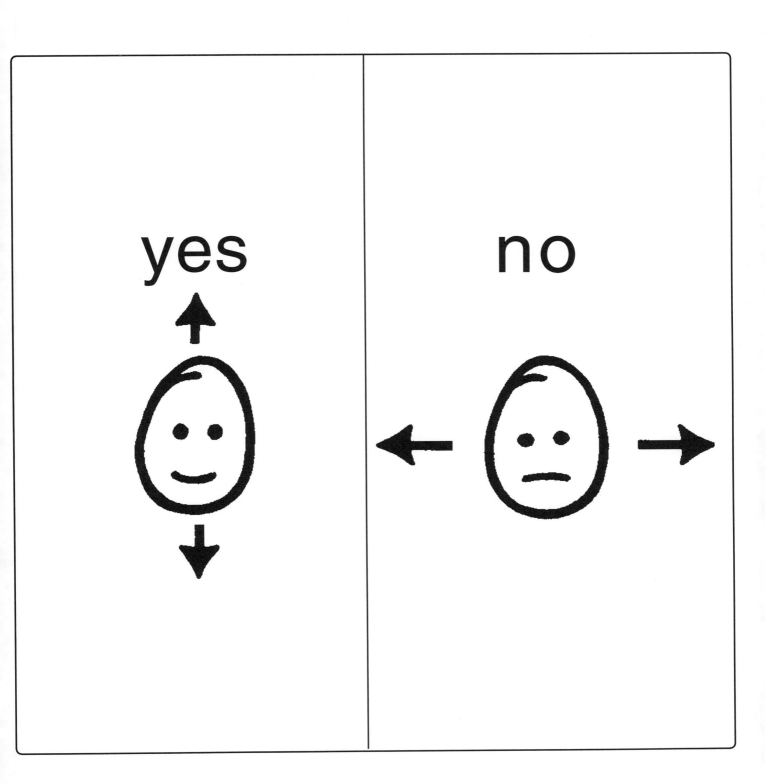

Grocery Store Unit

Categorizing Groceries

Grocery Store: Objective 1

Student will demonstrate categories necessary to correctly bag groceries.

Overview

There are specific rules for bagging groceries (see **Grocery Store**, Objective 3 for rules). Some of the rules vary from store to store, but one of the main requirements is for the person bagging to be able to quickly sort or categorize the grocery items and bag them accordingly. The following activities are designed to allow students to practice and refine these categorizing skills that will directly transfer to bagging groceries. The categories addressed are food and nonfood, cold and not cold, wet and dry, and paper or plastic. It is essential to use as many "real" items as possible when learning and practicing this skill. It is also important that students learn to stand while doing these activities since the job does not allow students to sit. Students should not be excluded from these activities just because they are not good candidates for a job in this area. Adaptations can be made to allow all students to benefit. Those who are not physically able to bag may be paired with more able-bodied students to learn the categorizing skills which will generalize to other types of jobs and to learn cooperative work skills.

Suggested Activities

Discriminate Food/Nonfood

Skill: *Discriminating between food and non-food.*
Activity: Using real items, discuss and practice discrimination of food and nonfood. Begin with obvious examples (bread and soap) and move toward more subtle differences (a box of crackers and a box of light bulbs). Use the **Food/Nonfood Overlay**, page 18, to practice this activity.

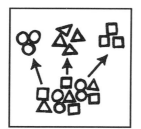

Practice Sorting By Categories

Skill: *Sorting grocery items by categories.*
Activity: Collect empty cans and boxes of food to practice sorting categories. Teach each category individually (wet/dry, cold/not cold, top/bottom, heavy/light, breakable/soft). As students become proficient in sorting, add more categories. Do this activity standing.

Paper Or Plastic?

Skill: *Asking customer if they want paper or plastic.*
Activity: Use real bags to practice asking the customer if he/she wants paper or plastic bags and practice correctly selecting paper or plastic in response to the customer's answer. Use the **Paper Or Plastic? Overlay**, page 19, to practice:
  • Asking the customer "paper or plastic?"
  • Responding appropriately by selecting the correct type of bag. Real grocery items can be used after initial training to com bine practice in asking what type of bag and correctly sorting and bagging.

Coupon Sorting

Skill: *Sorting coupons.*
Activity: Collect coupons from local papers. Students can cut out the coupons if able. Once cut out, it is helpful to laminate them so thay can be reused for practice. Then, with students in a standing position, they can use the coupons to sort into small lunch bags. Use the **Food/Nonfood, Paper or Plastic?, Cold/Not Cold, Wet/Dry Overlays,** pages 18-21, while doing this activity for additional practice. This can be made into a home/school activity by asking parents to send in coupons for items they often buy in their home. Students can match coupons to real items. Coupons can also be used in community shopping experiences.

Worksheet—Food/Nonfood
Using the worksheet on page 22, have students draw a line from the grocery item to the correct bag. With low students it is helpful to have the actual items that correspond with the symbols. Students may also cut out the item symbols and glue them onto the correct bag. Use the **Food/Nonfood Overlay**, page 18, while doing these worksheets. Cut out items for students unable to draw lines or cut and paste. They can then place/slide items to the correct bag or verbally (use overlays) indicate the correct placement of each item.

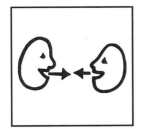

Vocabulary, Vocabulary, Vocabulary

The following are key vocabulary words for the **Grocery Store Unit**, Objective 1.

cold	wet	plastic
paper	food	nonfood
not cold	dry	

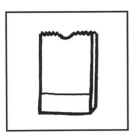

Generalization

Skill: *Sorting newspaper ads and coupons.*

Activity: Duplicate the **Grocery Store Activity Page,** page 23, for each student. (Label bags: food or nonfood, wet or dry, cold or not cold, etc.) For pictures, use local newspaper ads and coupons. *NOTE:* A good homework assignment is to ask the students to bring in ads from the stores where their families shop. Have students cut out grocery pictures or words and glue to the appropriate bag. Students who can write could write the words instead of cutting and pasting. This activity can easily be adapted for all students to complete. Use the **Food/Non-Food, Paper or Plastic?, Cold/Not Cold, Wet/Dry Overlays,** pages 18-21, as additional practice.

Worksheet — Cold/Not Cold

Using the worksheet on page 24, have students draw a line from the grocery item to the correct bag. With low students it is helpful to have the actual items that correspond with the symbols. Students may also cut out the item symbols and glue them onto the correct bag. Use the **Cold/Not Cold overlay,** page 20, while doing these worksheets. Cut out items for students unable to draw lines or cut and paste. They can then place/slide items to the correct bag or verbally (use overlays) indicate the correct placement of each item

Food/Nonfood Overlay

food

nonfood

Paper/Plastic Overlay

paper

plastic

Cold/Not Cold Overlay

Wet/Dry Overlay

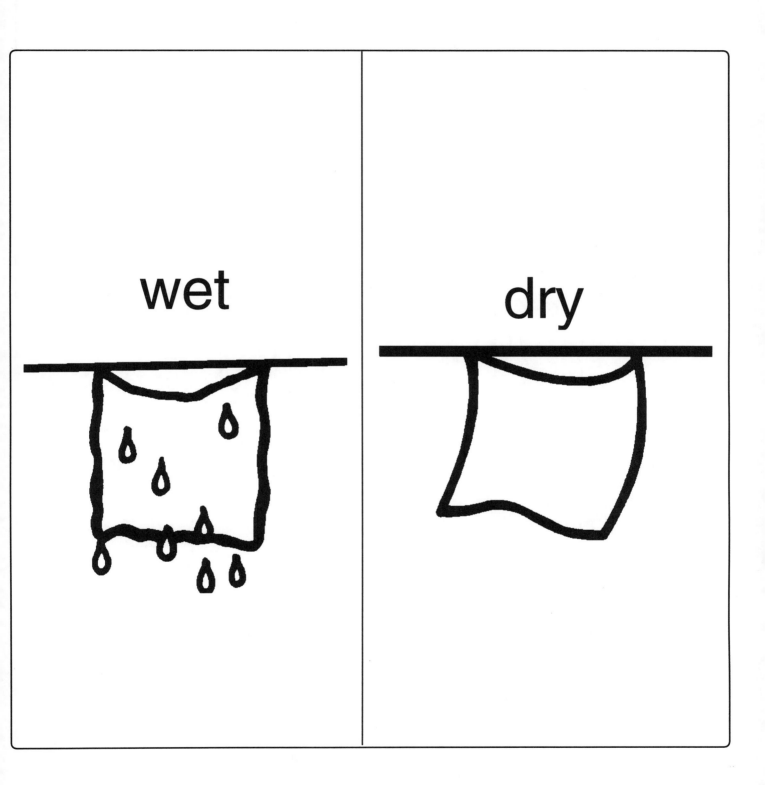

Worksheet
Food/Nonfood

Name _____ Date _____

Directions: Draw a line from each item to the correct bag.

spray

hot dog

milk
MILK

ketchup

soap
Dishwasher Soap

medicine
Rx

glass cleaner

chips
Chips

food

nonfood

Grocery Store Activity Page

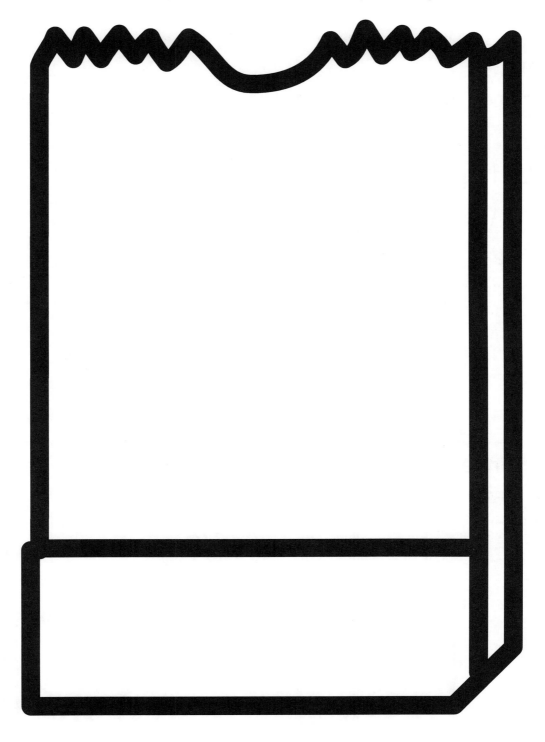

Teacher Directions: Duplicate one or two bags for each student. Label bag "food" or "nonfood" "wet or dry,"
etc. Have students cut out grocery pictures and/or coupons and glue onto the appropriate bag.

Grocery Store Unit

Worksheet
Cold/Not Cold

Name _____ Date _____

Directions: Draw a line from each item to the correct bag.

ketchup

meat

yogurt

peanut butter

ice cream

mayonnaise

fish sticks

baking soda

cold

not cold

"Face" (Straighten) Shelves

> ## Grocery Store: Objective 2
>
> *Student will demonstrate necessary skills to "face" (or straighten) shelves.*

Overview

In addition to bagging groceries, all grocery store employees are expected to help keep the store looking neat and appealing to customers. One of the major parts of this job is referred to as "facing" shelves. All food items are turned so that the labels are easily read and items are pulled to the front of the shelf so there are no empty spaces visible to the customer. The term "facing" may refer to the concept that the store desires to put on its best face for the customer. Facing requires good fine motor skills and eye-hand coordination. It should be practiced often and with real grocery items. Students who are physically unable to do the actual facing may be paired with other students to practice discrimination skills and communication skills.

Suggested Activities

What Is Facing?
Define facing with the student.

Skill: *Facing shelves.*

Activity: Set two display shelves to demonstrate a shelf that is neat and correctly faced and the other to demonstrate a shelf with items out of place. Discuss and correctly face the second shelf with the student. Use the **Yes/No Overlay**, page 13, to allow the student to respond "yes" or "no" to questions like:
- Is this shelf faced correctly?
- Do you see any items out of place?
- Is this item in the right place?

Review this activity often until the student can grasp the concept. Use library shelves or other shelves around the school to reinforce the concept. Point out shelves in stores on CBI trips.

Game

Skill: *Facing shelves.*

Activity: As a group, put grocery items on a shelf in the room and review the properties of a correctly faced shelf (labels turned to the front so they can be easily read, no empty spaces on the front of the shelf, no out-of-place items). Then have one or two students leave the room or turn their heads so they cannot see the shelf. Let the other students move items around so that the shelf is no longer correctly faced. Have the student return to the room and find the items incorrectly faced and correct them. This can be done individually or in teams. Be sure to use communication overlays to allow all students to participate. Vary the level of difficulty to match the students' ability.

Worksheet - Facing Shelves

Use these worksheets to review what a shelf should look like and to practice locating items out of place.

Practice, Practice, Practice

Skill: *Facing shelves.*

Activity: Collect empty cans of food with the labels still intact (or use full cans of food if available). Practice straightening, turning labels, etc. This skill cannot be practiced too much. It is an excellent eye-hand coordination activity.

I "Can" Do It

Skill: *Facing shelves.*

Activity: Collect empty soda cans and have students use them to "face" and shelve by brand names (Coke, Pepsi, Diet, Sprite, etc.). Make it a class project to collect cans and wash them. (HINT: Weight cans down with sand or Plaster of Paris so they do not tip over easily. Seal cans with tape or hot glue gun.) Allow students to help fill the drink machines at school. This is an excellent matching activity and a skill that transfers to many jobs.

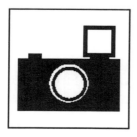

Pretty As A Picture

Skill: *Facing shelves.*

Activity: Take photos of a particular shelf faced correctly and then "mess up" the shelf. Have student reshelve and "face" like the photo.

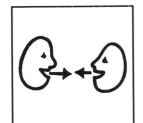

Vocabulary, Vocabulary, Vocabulary

The following are key vocabulary words for the **Grocery Store Unit**, Objective 2:

facing	shelf	can
bottle	glass	box

Generalization Activities

Skill: *Facing shelves.*

Activity: Have students unpack groceries at school and put on shelves. Ask parents to assist their children in practicing this skill at home. Point out correctly faced shelves in various places around the classroom and school building. Allow students to assist with any routine unpacking and storing tasks at school: janitorial supplies, lunchroom shelves, office supplies, storage items, library shelves. Use the term "facing" when referring to straightening the shelves. This term is used in most retail stores as well as grocery stores.

Worksheet - Facing Shelves, Yes/No Responses

Answering yes/no questions is very difficult for most students. It is also an essential skill for employment success. This worksheet is an opportunity to both practice the yes/no response and review facing rules.

Worksheet
Facing Shelves

Name _____ Date _____

Directions: Circle the one that goes on the shelf.

Worksheet
Facing Shelves, Yes/No Responses

Name _____ Date _____

Directions: Look at each shelf below. Circle "Yes" if it is faced correctly. Circle "No" if it is not faced correctly.

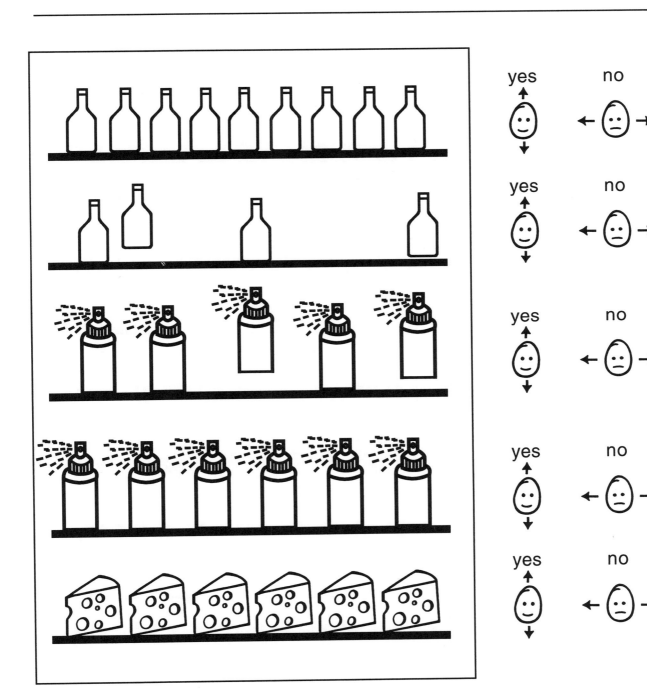

yes   no

yes   no

yes   no

yes   no

yes   no

Grocery Store Unit

Vocabulary Review

Name _____ Date _____

Directions: Write these words. Talk about what they mean and how you would use them.

_____

facing	
shelf	
can	
bottle	
glass	
box	

Bagging Groceries

Grocery Store: Objective 3
Student will demonstrate proper procedure for grocery bagging and transferring bagged items effectively (counter to cart to car).

Overview

Once the sorting and categorizing skills are developed, the student is ready to learn to actually bag groceries. This is a very difficult task which requires coordination and speed to do properly. Students should be allowed a great deal of time to practice, as these skills take time to master. Any opportunity to develop speed and coordination should be utilized. The general rules for bagging are listed on page 35. Specific stores may have variations on these rules, but the basic concepts are applicable to all major grocery store chains. In addition to bagging the groceries, the courtesy clerk must then safely transfer the bags from the counter to the cart (or customer's hands) and from the cart to the car if the customer requests assistance. This skill must also be practiced often.

Suggested Activities

Bag Groceries

Skill: *Bagging groceries.*
Activity: There is a written description of the basic bagging rules, page 35. Go over these with the students each time they practice. There is also a picture task analysis that can be used as a prompt or evaluation of the student, page 36. The key is to offer practice in as many situations as possible. Make the task as simple as necessary for each student. Use the **Bagging Groceries Overlay**, page 37, to practice communication skills.

Don't Squish Me!

Skill: *Bagging heavy/light and soft/not soft.*
Activity: This involves the concepts of heavy/light and soft/not soft. Using real grocery items (bread, chips, strawberries, etc.), show the students what happens when a heavy item is put on top. One of the

Don't Squish Me! (Continued)

major complaints from customers is that their bread or eggs were "squashed" by the courtesy clerk. Practice can be done as a yes/no activity (use the **Yes/No Overlay,** page 13) or a categorizing activity (use the **Food/Nonfood, Paper or Plastic?, Cold/Not Cold, Wet/Dry Overlays,** pages 18-21).

Worksheet—Bagging Groceries

Using the worksheet on page 38, have students pick out items that cannot go on the bottom of a grocery bag. Use real items for the discussion and then let students do the worksheet. As an alternative activity, copy the worksheet several times, laminate it, and cut the squares out. These can be used to play concentration type matching games (use the **Yes/No Overlay, page 13**).

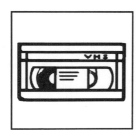

Video Madness

Skill: *Courtesy clerk training.*

Activity: Contact the managers of large chain stores and ask to see their training video for courtesy clerks or employees. Stores tend to be very possessive and/or suspicious of loaning their training materials. Be prepared to "sell" your need for the information. Sometimes you can borrow the videos, but more likely the manager will allow you to see it only on site. This would be a good culmination to a tour of the grocery stores or a unit on the various job possibilities in the grocery store. Major chains often have printed "rules" or guidelines for bagging. Enlist the manager's help in teaching these skills or at least in explaining them. Most stores have someone who loves to be "on" for groups. (Be sure to send a class thank-you note that involves the students - PR is essential.)

Class Store

Skill: *Bagging items and money handling.*

Activity: Set up a class "store." Have students earn money for completed tasks or for agreed amounts. Then they can use the money in the class "store" for goodies (candy, magazines, baseball cards, etc.). This allows practice in bagging items and can allow for practice of money handling skills also. The store can also be set up to be a practice grocery store (good for practicing facing skills). Video taping these sessions can be motivational and an excellent teaching tool. Use only real money! Play money really doesn't look anything like real money, especially to students who already have difficulty generalizing.

Practice, Practice, Practice

Skill: *Bagging groceries.*
Activity: Bring in real items and practice bagging groceries. Practice this skill often. To bag groceries effectively, the decisions must be automatic. There is not time to "think it through" while the groceries come down the conveyor belt. Be sure to practice with plastic as well as paper bags. Start with paper bags - they are much easier to handle. Local grocery stores will often give you bags and stands. Don't be afraid to ask. Use this opportunity to have students practice asking if the customer wants paper or plastic. Use the **Paper or Plastic? Overlay,** page 19, with this activity.

Be Careful With That Cart

Skill: *Maneuvering a grocery cart.*
Activity: Ask a local store if you can "borrow" a grocery cart to use in your classroom. If a grocery cart is not available, locate some type of wheeled device to approximate the task (a box tied to a hand truck makes a reasonable facsimile). Allow students to practice maneuvering in crowded areas. Set up an obstacle course with desks, shelves, or anything else available.

Loading The Bags

Skill: *Loading groceries.*
Activity: Fill grocery bags (be sure to use both paper and plastic). Have students practice lifting out and "loading" into a large box to simulate the trunk OR actually load into the teacher's car. This is an excellent time to practice parking lot safety!

Deliveries

Skill: *Delivering groceries.*
Activity: Have students make deliveries around school from the cart (mail, packages, books, notes, etc.). Offer to make purchases for other teachers when out on grocery store Community-Based Instruction trips. Allow the students to deliver these items from the cart. Use every opportunity possible to practice safe maneuvering and lifting.

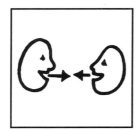

Vocabulary, Vocabulary, Vocabulary

The following are key vocabulary words for the **Grocery Store Unit**, Objective 3:

top	bottom	soft
eye contact	cart	load
bag groceries	heavy	light
not soft		

The Customer Is Always Right

Skill: *Eye contact and smiling.*

Activity: Stress eye contact and smiles. This is often a very difficult concept and behavior for students to learn. Practice and reinforce often. This is an essential skill for all jobs.

Task Analysis For Bagging Groceries

- [ ] Stand at the end of the checkout.
- [ ] Ask customers if they prefer paper or plastic bags.
- [ ] Open bags.
- [ ] Place cart behind you.
- [ ] Check customer's cart for large items (dog/cat food, 12 packs of soda, diapers, etc.)
- [ ] Load groceries into bags according to the following:
  - heavy items go on the bottom
  - frozen foods, cold foods go together
  - detergents, chemicals, nonfood items go together
  - breads, chips, cakes or produce go on top
  - eggs go into the bag laying down and on the bottom with something light on top
  - cans - no more than 8 to a bag
  - liter drinks - 2 to a bag, lying down
  - don't underfill or overfill a bag
  - magazines, cards bagged separately
  - bag ice cream in a separate bag
  - use boxes as sides of your bag standing upright
  - tie bags together holding smaller items (baby food jars)
  - don't bag:
    - 12 packs of drinks
    - diapers
    - already bagged fruits or vegetables
    - milk (ask customer if they want it bagged)
- [ ] Communicate with customer whether they need help bringing their groceries out to the car.
- [ ] Follow customer to car.
- [ ] Negotiate parking lot safely and appropriately.
- [ ] Communicate with customer where to put groceries.
- [ ] Place groceries gently into car/trunk in an upright position.
- [ ] Communicate an appropriate "thank you" for tip (if applicable).
- [ ] Renegotiate parking lot safely and appropriately.
- [ ] Return with cart to empty spot at the end of a checkout.

Picture Task Analysis For Bagging Groceries

 Get ready.

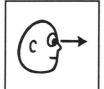 Look at the customer.

  Ask if he/she wants "pa-plastic?"

  Sort the food.

 Put the food in bags.

  Put the bags in the cart or give them to the customer.

  Put the bags in the car and say "goodbye."

Bagging Groceries Overlay

paper or plastic? 	How are you? 	May I help you? 
Where is your car? 	 Where do you want your bags?	Have a nice day! 
please 	thank you 	I need some help, please. 

Worksheet
Bagging Groceries

Name _____ Date _____

Directions: Put an X on the items that should <u>never</u> go on the bottom of the bag.

breakable	soft

cupcake	soda	Easter eggs

bread	doughnut	mayonnaise	meat	strawberry

chips		marshmallows		cake

banana	milk	hair spray	grapes	glass cleaner

Customer Interaction

Grocery Store: Objective 4

Student will demonstrate an awareness of the following appropriate interaction behaviors with customers:

Eye contact
Smiling
Responding to customer
Requesting/acquiring information
>   *Paper or plastic?*
>   *Do you need help?*
>   *Where is your car?*
>   *Where do you want your groceries?*

Social amenities
>   *Please*
>   *Thank you*
>   *Have a nice day*

Overview

Appropriate interaction with customers cannot be emphasized enough. Most complaints to the managers of grocery stores are about the poor treatment received from the courtesy clerks (poor bagging or rudeness). A pleasant disposition helps make up for limited skills. Students must learn to expect and be prepared for customers who will be angry and yell even if the student does everything right. It is essential that students internalize the concept that "**The customer is <u>always</u> right!**" These concepts are very abstract and difficult to teach in isolation. Always be on the lookout for naturally occurring opportunities for practice and discussion.

Suggested Activities

Role Play - Customer Interaction

Using the **Grocery Store Role Plays,** pages 42-45, practice/role play possible scenarios in the grocery store. Be sure to give students practice in dealing with angry or irrational customers and in responding to criticism by coworkers or the manager. This can be done as a group activity or made into a team game. Assign students a "character" in the role play script. Help them read and act out the parts (reading is not essential with adult assistance). Discuss the situations and alternatives/consequences.

Role Play - Customer Interaction (Continued)

Practice is the key and cannot be emphasized enough. Let students create their own role plays for each other once they learn to do them. Enlist the support of other adults to help the students generalize these skills. Don't forget to include appropriate communication overlays.

Video

Skill: *Customer relations.*
Activity: Most major chains have training films that emphasize customer relations. This is an excellent way to allow students to experience what the managers will be expecting and to see the importance of good work skills. These videos often must be viewed in the store.

Smiles Everyone

Skill: *Eye contact and smiles.*
Activity: Emphasize eye contact and smiles in all interactions at school. Engage other teachers or adults to practice this with your students.

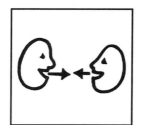

Vocabulary, Vocabulary, Vocabulary

The following are key vocabulary words for the **Grocery Store Unit**, Objective 4:

manager	customer	cold
eye contact	tip	wet
plastic	paper	bag groceries
soft	cart	soap
food	smile	nonfood
not cold	cashier	top
bottom	price	cans
dry		

Situation Cards

This activity is similar to role playing. Copy and cut apart the **Situation Cards,** pages 46-51. Glue these to 3 x 5 or 4 x 6 index cards. Laminate. Use these as a game, discussion starter, or even role play activities. One student could act out a response and the class could decide if it was appropriate or not. Use the **Yes/No Overlay,** page 13, for yes/no responses. Allow students to help you make up additional scenarios or talk to people who actually bag groceries and ask for their "horror" stories. Practice is important! This is an excellent time to enlist peers in the school who actually work in grocery stores. Peers have more influence than adults.

Worksheet—Bagging Groceries 1 & 2

Use these worksheets, pages 52-53, as discussion pages or seat work. They also make great homework sheets to help parents see what the student is learning. Students circle the correct answer to the question. This activity provides a great discussion opportunity. Students fill in the blanks - they can write the word in or cut and paste the symbol.

Worksheet—Vocabulary Review 1-7

Copy the worksheets, pages 54-60, that are appropriate for the student's ability level - copying words without symbols, copying words with symbols, a few words on a page, or several words on a page. This list can also be used for review of vocabulary and discussion words.

Role Play: Paper Or Plastic?

This role play will require two characters, a courtesy clerk and a customer. An additional character could be a cashier. Props should include groceries, paper and plastic bags, a cart, something to represent the trunk of a car, and a tip.

Courtesy Clerk: Would you like paper or plastic?

Customer: Plastic, please.

Courtesy Clerk: How are you today?

Customer: My back hurts, and I have had a headache all day.

Courtesy Clerk: (*Bagging groceries with plastic bags.*) I'm sorry to hear that. I hope you will feel better soon.

Customer: Hey, I told you to use paper bags. You're using plastic. I hate plastic.

Courtesy Clerk: Oh, I must have misunderstood. I'll get these in paper right away. (*Re-bags groceries in paper bags.*) May I take these to your car?

Customer: Yes, please, I am too tired to do it myself.

Courtesy Clerk: (*Follows customer to car, pushing cart.*) Should I put these in the back seat or the trunk?

Customer: The trunk, please. Here, I'll open it for you.
(*Opens trunk.*)

Courtesy Clerk: (*Unloads groceries into trunk and closes the lid.*) There you go.

Customer: Thank you for your help.
(*Hands courtesy clerk a tip.*)

Courtesy Clerk: Thank YOU! Have a nice day.

Role Play: New Job

(Thursday afternoon, aisle 7 at the grocery store.)

Mrs. Smith: Well! Hello, Susan. I didn't know you were working here at the grocery store.

Susan: Yeah, I just got the job yesterday, but I don't like it very much. It is really boring.

Mrs. Smith: You don't like it? Why not?

Susan: Well, I hardly ever get to see Jason, my boyfriend. Oh, there he is now. Hi, sweetie!

Jason: Hi, Susan. How's it going?

Susan: Just awful! Look at all these groceries I have to bag. And look, she even bought the kind of peas I hate - they make me throw up.

Mrs. Smith: Oh, Susan, I don't think you're supposed to put the canned peas on top of the potato chips.

Susan: Chill out, Mrs. Smith, there's plenty of room in the bag!

Mrs. Smith: *(Angry.)* I'm going to find the manager to see if I can get someone to bag my groceries who knows what they are doing!

Questions:

1. Should Susan visit with her boyfriend during work?

2. Should Susan discuss how she feels about the customer's food?

3. What was wrong with the way Susan was bagging the peas and the potato chips?

4. Do you think Mrs. Smith will give Susan a tip? Why or why not?

Role Play: The Unhappy Customer

Courtesy Clerk: Would you like paper or plastic?

Customer: I don't care, just don't put all the cans in one bag. I hate that.

Courtesy Clerk: Yes, ma'am (or sir).
(*Bags groceries in plastic bag.*)

Customer: And don't put anything in the same bag as my chicken. I hate it when the chicken drips all over everything. Do you understand?

Courtesy Clerk: Oh, yes, I'll be very careful of your chicken.

Customer: The last time I was here the bagger put the chicken in with my cereal. The cereal box was ruined. I brought it back and told the manager he should fire that person. Someone that stupid has no business with a job.

Courtesy Clerk: I'll try to be very careful. We want happy customers.

Questions:

1. Why do you think this customer is acting so angry with the courtesy clerk?

2. What would probably happen if the courtesy clerk was rude to this customer?

3. What is the correct way to bag any cold food or meats?

4. Should cereal and chicken ever be put in the same grocery bag?

Role Play: The Boss Is Always Right

The courtesy clerk is stocking shelves in the canned vegetable aisle. His manager walks up and begins to watch him work.

Courtesy Clerk: Good morning, sir (or ma'am).

Manager: Good morning. What are you doing?

Courtesy Clerk: I am stocking. I have two cases of canned beans to put up and then there is another rolling rack of vegetables to put out.

Manager: The beans do not go in this section. They go down at the end of the aisle.

Courtesy Clerk: Yes, sir, they usually do, but Mr. Jones told me to put these beans here for a special display.

Manager: I don't care what Mr. Jones told you. I do not want the beans to go there. Now move them immediately. I'll take care of Mr. Jones.

Courtesy Clerk: Yes, sir, you're the boss.

Questions:

1. Should the courtesy clerk tell Mr. Jones what happened or keep quiet and let Mr. Jones find out for himself?

2. What may have happened if the courtesy clerk had tried to argue with the manager about what Mr. Jones had told him to do?

3. Why is it important to be polite to the boss even when you disagree?

Grocery Store Situation Cards

Sean, the stock person, is putting out cans of beans. The manager passes him and says, "No, you have to put corn there. Take all the beans off."

What should Sean do?

1. Quit and go out to lunch.

2. Take down all the beans and put out corn.

3. Get a broom and sweep the front sidewalk.

Mary is on her way to bag groceries in the front of the store when she hears a crash followed by the sound of glass breaking. A large jar of pickles has been knocked off the shelf and shattered.

Mary should:

1. Stay and warn customers away, and send the next employee she sees for help.

2. Go on to the bagging job - this is none of her business.

3. Leave and get a broom to clean up the mess.

Grocery Store Situation Cards

Jerry begins to bag the customer's groceries without asking if he/she wants paper or plastic. Putting groceries in plastic bags is easier for Jerry so he automatically starts bagging with plastic bags. The customer wants paper and yells at Jerry for using plastic.

What should Jerry do?

1. Throw down the bag and walk away.

2. Call the customer names.

3. Apologize and re-bag the groceries even though it makes him mad.

Mary is bagging groceries. She accidentally puts a heavy jar of pickles on top of a loaf of bread. The bread is mashed flat.

Mary should:

1. Say, "I'm sorry," and send another worker to get another loaf of bread.

2. Leave it and keep bagging.

3. Take the pickles out and put them in another bag.

Grocery Store Unit

Grocery Store Situation Cards

Bill is bagging Mrs. Smith's groceries. She only has two things: a package of raw hamburger and a can of bug spray.

Bill should:

1. Put them both in the same bag.

2. Put them in separate bags.

3. Put only the bug spray in a bag, and hand the hamburger to Mrs. Smith to carry.

Mr. Jones is buying three things: ice cream, milk, and shampoo.

Janet, the courtesy clerk, should:

1. Put the milk and shampoo together.

2. Put all three items in the same bag.

3. Put the milk and the ice cream together and bag the shampoo separately.

Grocery Store Situation Cards

Johnny just got through bagging Mr. Black's groceries. Mr. Black did not want any help taking them to his car. It is time for Johnny's morning break. The cashier asks him to do a price check for her.

Johnny should:

1. Tell the cashier that he cannot help her, it is break time.

2. Quickly do the price check and then go on break.

3. Ask another courtesy clerk to help the cashier.

Fran gets to work at the grocery store and realizes that she has left her name tag at home. The store has a very strict policy about wearing your name tag.

Fran should:

1. Call her mother to bring her name tag.

2. Tell her supervisor that she needs another name tag.

3. Pretend like she doesn't notice her name tag is missing.

Grocery Store Situation Cards

It is Lonnie's turn to retrieve shopping carts from the parking lot. The store policy is never to push more than four carts together at one time. Lonnie has seen other courtesy clerks pushing many more carts and it looked easy.

What should Lonnie do?

1. Go ahead and try to push as many carts as possible.

2. Follow the store policy and only push four carts at a time.

3. Tell the manager that the other courtesy clerks are not following the policy.

Alice just finished bagging Mrs. Lord's groceries. Mrs. Lord said she would like Alice to help her with the groceries, and they start out the front door to Mrs. Lord's car. Just as they leave the store, Mrs. Lord meets a neighbor and they stop to talk. Alice gets tired of waiting for Mrs. Lord to finish.

Alice should:

1. Keep walking and hope that Mrs. Lord will notice and follow her.

2. Tell Mrs. Lord to hurry up because she must go back to work.

3. Wait patiently on Mrs. Lord to finish.

Grocery Store Situation Cards

Danny works at BIG C Grocery. He usually clocks in with an electronic clock. Today the time clock is broken and the employees must sign in on a time sheet. Danny does not have a watch.

What should Danny do?

1. Ask another employee what time it is.

2. Sign his name, but not write a time.

3. Write down what time he is supposed to start work even though he does not know what time it really is.

Tracy fell after work and skinned her knee and elbow badly. When she got up the next morning, her knee and elbow were stiff and sore.

Tracy should:

1. Call in to work and say that she does not feel well.

2. Go to work and show everyone her sores.

3. Get help in covering the scraped areas with bandages and go on to work.

Worksheet 1
Bagging Groceries

Name _____ Date _____

Directions: Circle the best answer.

1. When Fred bags Mrs. Smith's groceries, what should he do first?

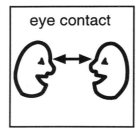 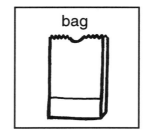 

2. Before Fred begins to bag, he will ask...

3. Which one of these would Fred put in the same bag with chicken?

4. When he's finished bagging the groceries, Fred will say...

Worksheet 2
Bagging Groceries

Name _____ Date _____

Directions: Circle the best answer.

___

1. When Mrs. Smith gives Fred a tip, he will say...

2. Which of these items can go on the bottom of a grocery bag?

3. Which of these cannot go on the bottom of a grocery bag?

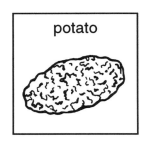

4. It is very important to......when working in public.

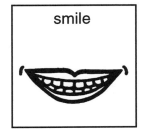

Grocery Store Unit

Worksheet 1
Vocabulary Review

Name _____ Date _____

Directions: Use the words below to fill in the blanks:

manager	customer	cold	eye contact	tip	wet

1. If a courtesy clerk takes a customer's bags to his/her car and does a good job, the customer might give a ⬚ .

2. If a worker in a grocery store is not sure of something, the ⬚ is the person to ask.

3. A good courtesy clerk will make ⬚ with the customer.

4. The ⬚ is always right

5. Milk, ice cream, and frozen peas are ⬚ items.

6. Copy these words:

manager

_____

customer

_____

eye contact

_____

cold

_____

wet

_____

tip

_____

Worksheet 2
More Vocabulary Review

Name _____ Date _____

Directions: Use the words below to fill in the blanks:

_____

plastic	paper	bag groceries	soft	cart	soap

1. Some bags are made of [ ] and some are made of [ ].

2. Groceries are bagged and then loaded into a [ ].

3. [ ] items are <u>never</u> put on the bottom of a grocery bag.

4. One job of a courtesy clerk is to [ ].

5. [ ] should <u>never</u> go in the same bag with fruits and vegetables.

Grocery Store Unit

Worksheet 3
Vocabulary Review

Name _____ Date _____

Directions: These words are important to know if you work in a grocery store. Talk about what each word means. Write each word for practice.

food

smile

_____ _____

nonfood

bag groceries

_____ _____

plastic

paper

_____ _____

cold

not cold

_____ _____

wet

dry

_____ _____

Worksheet 4
Vocabulary Review

Name _____ Date _____

Directions: These words are important to know if you work in a grocery store. Talk about what each word means. Write each word for practice.

cashier

_____

manager

_____

bottom

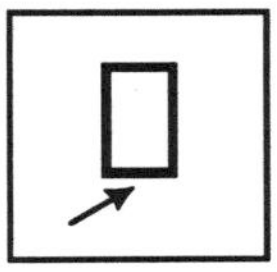

_____

customer

_____

cans

_____

top

_____

eye
contact

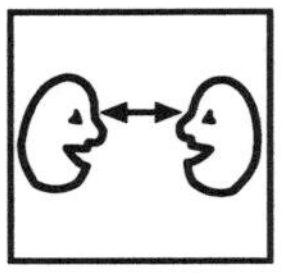

_____

price

_____

soft

_____

Grocery Store Unit

Worksheet 5
Vocabulary Review

Name _____ Date _____

Directions: Match the words to the correct symbol. Then write the word.

top	smile	
bottom	eye contact	
wet	cold	
dry	top	
smile	food	
(eye contact)	bottom	
food	dry	
cold	wet	

Worksheet 6
Vocabulary Review

Name _____ Date _____

Directions: Match the words to the correct symbol. Then write the word.

Symbol	Word	Write
plastic bag	smile	
cold	cashier	
paper bag	cart	
bag groceries	manager	
cashier	paper bag	
manager	plastic bag	
not cold	cold	
cart	not cold	

Vocabulary Review

Name _____ Date _____

Directions: These words are important to know if you work in a grocery store.
Talk about what each word means and then write them for practice.

manager _____	bagging _____	food _____
cold _____	not cold _____	nonfood _____
price _____	paper bag _____	plastic bag _____
cart _____	cashier _____	tip _____
eye contact _____	customer _____	smiles _____

Personal Appearance

Grocery Store: Objective 5

Student will demonstrate an understanding of the importance of personal appearance in the workplace: Uniforms/ appropriate clothes, grooming, appropriate accessories (jewelry, hats, bandanas, etc.).

Overview

Having the necessary skills to perform a job and keeping the job are two different matters. Students need to develop a sense of pride in their appearance as well as in their work. It is a difficult task for most teenagers to grasp that they cannot make all the decisions where dress and appearance are concerned. Employers are very conscious of the public image of their employees, especially in such a service job as courtesy clerk. Proper appearance should be taught as an essential skill, just as categorizing or bagging.

Suggested Activities

Ready For Work or Not Ready For Work?

Skill: *Personal appearance.*
Activity: Use the **Ready For Work Discussion Pictures**, pages 63 & 64, to begin the students thinking about what is appropriate and inappropriate for the work setting, especially in the grocery store. Make a list of what is "right" or "wrong" with each picture.

Poster Session

Skill: *Identifying appropriate and inappropriate work clothes.*
Activity: Have students make posters - one half would be appropriate work clothes and the other half would be clothes you cannot wear to work. Use the terms appropriate and inappropriate. Use the posters as discussion starters.

Worksheet—Appropriate And Inappropriate Workplace Attire
Use this worksheet, page 65, to identify appropriate and inappropriate attire at the workplace. Stress that not coming to work dressed appropriately can mean a loss of the job and therefore the paycheck. Worksheets can be laminated and cut apart for a more hands-on task.

The Real World

Skill: *Following work dress codes.*
Activity: Contact your local grocery stores and find out what their employee dress codes are. Discuss these with the students. Make a poster with each of the rules listed and have the students find pictures to show the correct and incorrect way to follow the dress code rules.

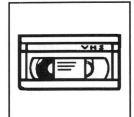

Videos

Skill: *Personal appearance.*
Activity: Again, most major chains include personal appearance emphasis in their training videos. You may have to view the video at the store.

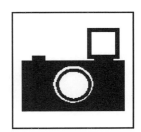

A Picture Is Worth A Thousand Words

Skill: *Correct uniform or work attire.*
Activity: Get permission from the local grocery store(s) to take pictures of their employees in correct uniform or work attire. This is a good way to show that not all jobs have the exact same requirements, but that there are some basic things that are the same. Use a camera or video camera to let students model correct and incorrect attire (messy hair vs. combed hair, shaven vs. unshaven, clean clothes vs. messy/dirty clothes, too much jewelry, high heels, etc.).

The Voice Of Experience

Skill: *Importance of personal appearance.*
Activity: Schedule store managers or other grocery store employees to come talk to the class about the importance of personal appearance. Have them explain their store's policy and what happens to violators. Video tape this presentation if the manager is willing.

Worksheet - Getting Ready For Work
Students are asked to cut out symbols and place in the correct location. 'Yes' if you <u>should</u> do this to get ready for work and 'No' if you <u>do not</u> need to do this to get ready for work.

Ready For Work Discussion Picture

Grocery Store Unit

Not Ready For Work Discussion Picture

Worksheet
Ready For Work/Not Ready For Work

Name _____ Date _____

Directions: Draw a line from each item to the correct box.

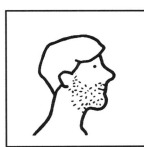

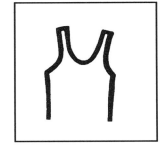

Grocery Store Unit

Worksheet
Getting Ready For Work

Name _____ Date _____

Directions: Cut apart the symbols at the bottom of the page and glue them under the correct box.

| yes | "Yes", if you <u>should</u> do this to get ready for work. | no | "No", if you <u>do not</u> need to do this to get ready for work. |

yes	no

walkman	look in mirror	bathe	brush teeth	cap	facial hair

deodorant	scarf	iron	brush hair	make-up	name tag

Community Experience

The skills taught and practiced in the classroom and school setting must be generalized to the community. The following are possibilities for community experiences:

Tour of local grocery stores

- Contact the manager of your nearby grocery store. Usually, managers are willing to set up a tour of the meat, bakery, deli, and produce departments.

- National chains usually have terrific training videos on a variety of topics. Bagging, stocking, cleanup, cash register operation, and general hiring practices are usually covered. Ask the manager if you can set up a time to view films in the store, or even allow you to borrow the films to show in class.

- Ask the manager if some of your students can observe some courtesy clerks bagging. Point out the techniques that you have practiced in the classroom. Some kind clerk may even allow you to try some bagging. Remember that some courtesy clerks work for tips, and many are dependent upon these for income. If your student is given a tip, direct the student to offer the tip to the clerk. Don't "clump" - if you are observing at a grocery store, take only one or two students. Make arrangements to leave the others at school or have other students in another area of the store.

Locate correctly and incorrectly faced shelves at any store

Walk students up and down the aisles and ask them "What do you think about this one?" Point out examples of correctly and incorrectly faced shelves. Get clearance from the manager before having the students face shelves.

Volunteer to work in a local library

Ask the head librarian if your students can get a demonstration of book shelving procedures. You may even be able to get permission to have the students shelve books. Watch carefully and check the students' work. Stress the importance of having the books in the appropriate places for ease in location.

Retail Unit

Retail Unit

Vocational opportunities in a retail store are excellent possibilities for learners with special needs. In this unit, students are introduced to skills important to workers in retail sales situations. These include stockroom skills such as:

- Safe lifting and stacking practices
- Pricing
- Folding and hanging merchandise
- Preparing merchandise for display
- Stocking items and returned merchandise

Support materials for this unit include a variety of communication overlays specific to these tasks, worksheets on several levels, data collection and assessment forms, as well as a listing of vocabulary words and related concepts. Also included are forms designed to foster communication between school and home. Objectives for this unit include:

Objective 1: *Hanging up clothing (page 83).*
Objective 2: *Unpacking and packing merchandise items (page 95).*
Objective 3: *Pricing merchandise (page 111).*
Objective 4: *Stocking shelves (page 121).*
Objective 5: *Trash disposal (page 145).*
Objective 6: *Carrying and lifting procedures (page 159).*

There are standard forms and overlays that are used for each objective. These include:

Vocational Update Letter to Parents — Use this form to send home with the student before the unit objective begins. It will give the parent or caregiver an overview of the unit objective plus extend the activity into the home, (see page 72).

Calendar of Skills — Home activities that help reinforce skills learned in school, (see page 73).

Vocabulary Words — Common vocabulary words used throughout the four objectives, (see page 74).

Evaluation/Documentation Forms — Use these forms to assess goal achievement and/or formulate IEP goals and objectives (see pages 75-78).

Same/Different Overlay — Simple overlay used with many of the unit objectives (see page 79).

Same/Different and Yes/No Overlay — A four choice overlay used with many of the unit objectives (see page 80).

Yes/No Overlay - A two choice overlay used with several of the unit objectives (see page 81).

Vocational Update

Dear Parents,

In class, we are working on a unit to learn skills important to working in a store.

These are some vocabulary words we are using:

These are some activities you might want to try at home:

Thank you for your support in this important learning experience. Please sign and return.

Very truly yours,

_____

Parent signature _____

Calendar of Skills

Let your child fold and put away towels. Fold towels into long thirds, short quarters.

Sticker Fun! When pricing items, price tags often have to be in a specific place and always right side up. Purchase an inexpensive pack of stickers and have your child practice sticking them on newspaper pages. You pick the spot.

With your child, make a list of 15 things you can find in a department store that you can't find in a grocery store.

Wash windows!!! Stores often have windows and glass that has to be polished. Use a spray bottle and paper towels or newspaper. Watch for streaks!

Talk about manners and why it is important to be polite to customers

Talk about these questions:

"Why should you call your boss if you are not coming in to work?"

"What are some good/bad reasons for not going to work?"

Have your child hang up shirts making sure they button up the front and hang up all facing the same direction. You might want to start with T-shirts.

Put away the dishes. Have your child line up glasses, plates, bowls, neatly in the cabinets.

Have your child remove all items from a shelf or counter. Wipe systematically with cloth and mild cleaner, then replace items neatly.

Organize your linen closet!!! Have your child fold and make stacks of towels, washcloths, sheets, pillow cases, etc. Label shelves and arrange.

Parents,
Above is a suggested calendar of skills for our unit on Retail Store jobs. Please try to do seven out of ten of these activities with your child to enrich our work at school. Initial the skills you are able to complete and return the list by _____ : Students who return the calendar with seven of ten items initialed will receive _____ .

Thank you for your support,

_____

Vocabulary Words - Retail Unit

hang	garment	foamies	stretch
hanger	size	left	neck
clothes	straight	shoulder pads	count
same	more	fold	help
box	trash	stack	trash can
carry	price	hanger	bottom
stock number	store	front	stockroom
truck	inventory	shopback	department
loading dock	merchandise	right	left
down	up	match	recycle
cardboard	retail store	boxes	compactor
breakdown	clean up	empty	sort
safety	trash bag		

Evaluation/Documentation

The evaluation and documentation instruments are included to help the teacher track the skills each student has attempted. They can be helpful when assessing goal achievement and formulating IEP goals and objectives. There are two different evaluation forms. The teacher may choose to use one or the other or both, depending on the needs of the class.

Retail Store
IEP Goals and Objectives

The student will. . .

☐ Demonstrate the ability to select correct type of hanger and appropriately hang various types of clothing.

☐ Demonstrate necessary skills to carefully unpack and repack items.
    ☐ fold / unfold
    ☐ count items
    ☐ clean items (removing unnecessary paper/plastic)
    ☐ replace "cleaned" items in packing case
    ☐ open sealed boxes (boxcutter, scissors, etc.)

☐ Demonstrate necessary skills to price merchandise
    ☐ use a price gun
    ☐ use price stickers
    ☐ place stickers appropriately

☐ Demonstrate ability to stock shelves
    ☐ match same color/style/size
    ☐ match stock numbers
    ☐ display merchandise appropriately
    ☐ recover/shopback - return merchandise to appropriate location

☐ Demonstrate appropriate trash disposal skills
    ☐ keep work area free of trash
    ☐ sort cardboard/plastic/paper
    ☐ break down boxes and using a compactor
    ☐ empty trash

☐ Demonstrate safe carrying and lifting practices
    ☐ recognize correct/incorrect lifting procedures
    ☐ two person lift
    ☐ appropriate use of back-support belts (OSHA regulations)
    ☐ stack and retrieve boxes safely
    ☐ use stock numbers to locate and store boxes

Evaluation Documentation Grocery Store Unit
Individual Student Format

Objectives	worksheet	worksheet	worksheet	practice	worksheet	activity	activity	community	overlay	overlay		
Student's Name _____												
1. Correct Hanger Selection.												
2. Necessary folding & unfolding skills												
fold / unfold												
count items												
clean items (removing paper/plastic)												
replace "cleaned" items in cases												
open sealed boxes												
3. Necessary skills to price merchandise												
use a price gun												
use price stickers												
place stickers appropriately												
4. Ability to stock shelves												
match same color/style/size												
match stock numbers												
display merchandise appropriately												
recover/shopback merchandise												
return merchandise to correct location												
5. Appropriate trash disposal skills												
keep work area free of trash												
sort cardboard/plastic/paper												
break down boxes and use compactor												
empty trash												
6. Safe carrying and lifting practices												
recognize correct/incorrect lifting procedures												
two person lift												
appropriate use of back-support belts												
stack and retrieve boxes safely												
use stock numbers to locate and store boxes												

Evaluation Documentation: Retail Unit
Total Class Format

Objectives	students														
1. Correct hanger selection & hanging techniques															
Sorting hangers by size & style															
Selecting correct hangers to use															
Hanging clothes on hangers correctly															
2. Demonstrate ability to unpack & repack items															
Counting items & writing numbers down															
Using correct techniques to fold clothes															
Cleaning items (remove paper, etc.)															
Replacing cleaned items in cases															
Opening sealed boxes (boxcutters, etc.)															
3. Demonstrate necessary skills for pricing															
Using a price gun															
Using price stickers															
Placing stickers appropriately															
4. Demonstrate ability to stock shelves															
Matching same color, styles & stock numbers															
Displaying merchandise appropriately															
Recovering/returning shopbacks															
D. Demonstrate appropriate trash disposal skills															
Sorting cardboard/plastic/paper															
Breaking down boxes & using compactors															
Emptying the trash															
E. Demonstrate safe carrying/lifting techniques															
Recognizing/using correct lifting procedures															
Appropriate use of back-support belts															
Stacking/retrieving boxes safely															
Using stocknumbers to locate & store boxes															

Same/Different Overlay

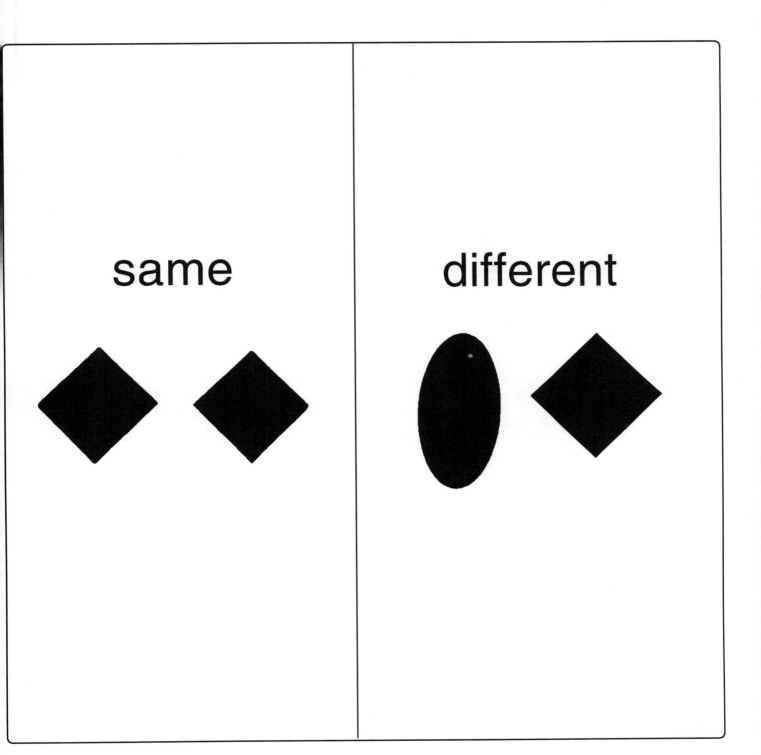

Same/Different and
Yes/No Overlay

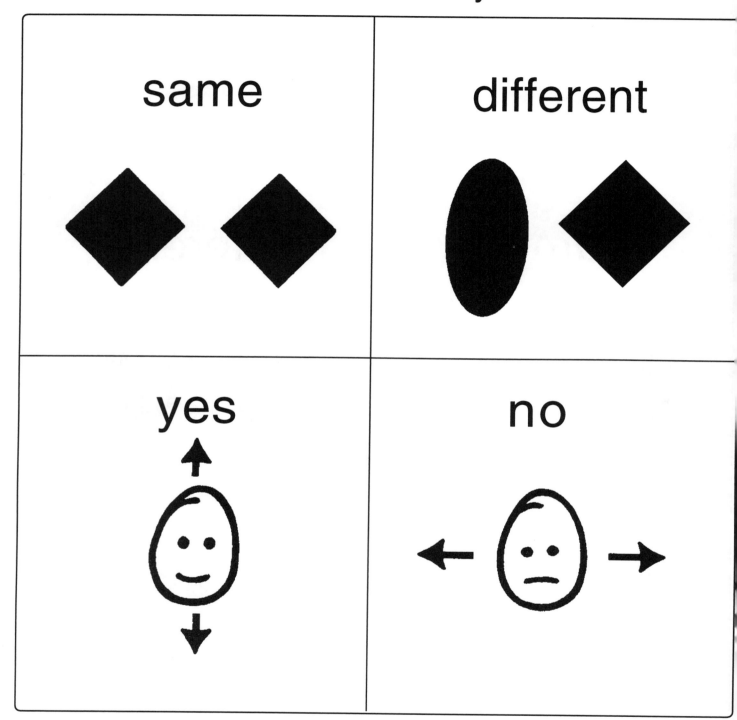

same

different

yes

no

Yes / No Overlay

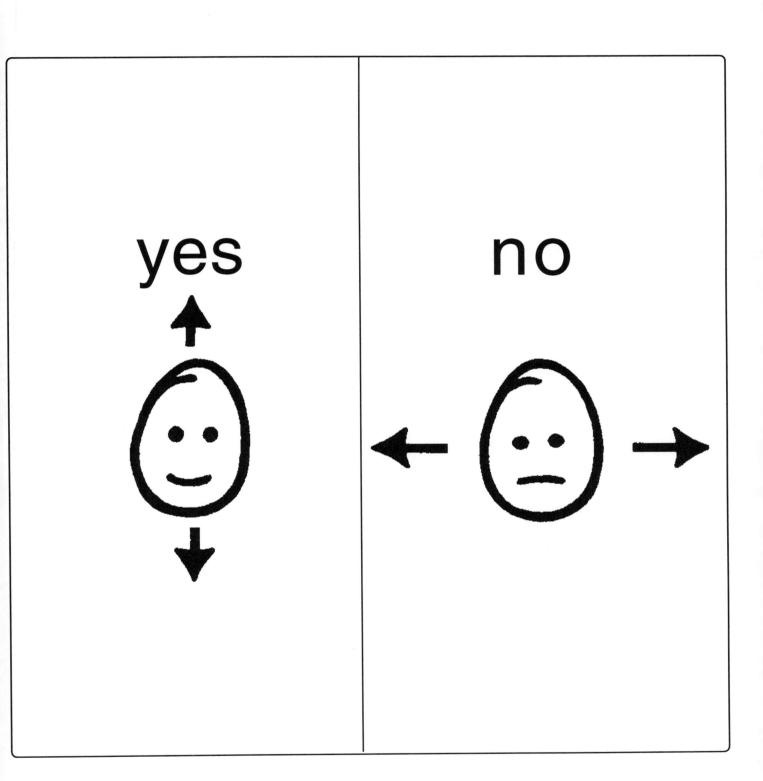

Retail Store Unit

Hanging Up Clothes

Retail Store: Objective 1

Student will demonstrate the ability to select correct type of hanger and appropriately hang various types of clothing.

Overview

Each retail store has specific requirements for hanging garments. There are rules as to how garments are hung and on what type of hangers. Many stores take the clothes off the hangers they come shipped on and use more sturdy store hangers. Often, the shipping hangers are plastic and the hook portion is stationary which limits the flexibility in display and hanging space. Generally, clothing for women and girls are hung on white or clear hangers, clothing for men and boys are hung on black hangers, and small children's clothing is hung on smaller hangers. In addition to selecting the correct type of hanger, workers must be able to sort hangers since they are usually dropped into a bin or other container at the checkout for reuse. Workers are dispatched to various departments to retrieve hangers for the receiving area to use for hanging new merchandise. Another important skill is correctly hanging various types of clothes:

- Hangers go up from the bottom instead of through the neck.
- Shoulder pads must be on hanger straight.
- Women's pants are generally hung "open" while men's pants are generally hung folded closed.

It is essential to provide adequate practice materials to develop these skills. Hanging up one's coat is a good way to make the skill functional, but it will not provide the necessary practice needed to develop endurance and speed. Students should not be excluded from these activities just because they are not good candidates for a job in this area. Adaptations can be made to allow all students to benefit. Those who are not physically able to actually hang may be paired with more able-bodied students to partially participate or tasks can be broken down for partial participation (handing a hanger to another student).

Suggested Activities

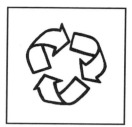

Recycle, Recycle, Recycle

For this unit objective, you will need a large number of items that are not usually in a classroom. Send home a request letter before this unit begins asking for used items or donations. Don't forget to ask fellow teachers for help. Items you need to collect are:

- Old T-shirts.
- Any type of old clothes to hang and/or practice folding (you will want a variety of styles, sizes, colors, etc.).
- Hangers—as many different colors and styles as possible.

In addition to asking parents and teachers, you may also wish to contact local merchants and ask if they have any hangers they would donate, or ask for the plastic hangers they throw away. Although these are not the type of hangers most stores use on the display floor, they will provide the students with practice and that is important.

Sort Hangers By Size And Style

Many retail stores keep the hangers when a customer buys an item and toss them into a box at the cash register. Later stock personnel sort the hangers and reuse them to hang new merchandise.

Skill: *Sorting new clothing merchandise. (Can come folded or with plastic covering item(s).)*
Activity: Have students sort clothes onto a hanging rack of some type (spring shower rods work well stretched across a door).

Skill: *Untangling hangers—used hangers tangle a great deal when they are just tossed into a box.*
Activity: Have students untangle the hangers. This is an excellent eye-hand coordination for the students (and often frustration tolerance). You should have a minimum of 100 hangers.

This job requires patience, endurance, and a lot bending and stretching. Pair students who cannot do the job independently. Remember partial participation is critical. Try to include as many different types of hangers as possible—see **Types of Hangers Discussion Picture** on page 90, for reference.

For the hanger sorting activity, use **Same/Different Overlay** or **Same/Different and Yes/No Overlay**, pages 79 & 80. Any overlay that has a yes/no response will be effective in this activity.

Hanger Selection — Which One Do I Use Now?

This is a familiar question in a stockroom for new employees. Each store has its own particular method of hanging items, but there are some standard guidelines that will help students make decisions.

Skill: *Identifing incorrectly hung clothing.*
Activity: Hang the garments on incorrect hangers; e.g., shirt on pants hanger, men's shirt on child's hanger, etc. (use the materials from the previous sorting activity for this activity). Discuss why the hanger won't work. Have students identify the correct hanger needed. This can be done as an individual, small group, or team activity. Use the **Hanger Identification Overlay,** page 90 and/or **Hanging Clothes Discussion Picture,** page 91, for this activity.

Worksheet 1 and 2 — Hanger Selection

Students can practice matching clothing to hangers using the **Hanger Selection Worksheet 1 and 2,** pages 88-89. Use **Same/Different Overlay**, page 79 and/or **Same/Different and Yes/No Overlay**, page 80, during this activity.

Don't Stretch The Neck!

Shirts and blouses are usually hung from the bottom instead of through the neck. Even shirts with buttons are hung this way because it takes too much time to unbutton and rebutton while hanging. **DO NOT** STRETCH THE HANGER THROUGH THE NECK.

Skill: *Hanging T-shirts on hangers correctly.*
Activity 1: Provide students with a box of 24 or more similar type T-shirts (the more you have, the more like a job simulation this will be). Have students hang the shirts correctly by inserting hanger from the bottom of the shirt, then hang the shirt on a rack (see shower curtain rod idea under **Sort Hangers,** page 84.

Activity 2: Sort hangers by size and style. Provide students with a variety of hangers. Have students separate hangers into boxes according to hanger size and/or hanger style. This task should be done standing, not sitting, if at all possible. Remember that no one gets to sit down while he/she works.

Rules To Hang By

Once the act of hanging is mastered, focus on hanging clothing so that all the shirts hang the same way:

- Buttons or front of shirts all face the same way. TIP: It's helpful to have them select a specific reference item such as a wall or piece of furniture to turn all the shirts toward.

- Hanger hooks always hang OVER the hook from the front, not the back.
  TIP: A good rule of thumb is to have the hanger hook face to the left when you look at the front of the shirt.

- Practice hanging like shirts together. This can be done by color, style, or size. TIP: Once one type of sorting is mastered, change to another type.

Students who are physically unable to hang the shirts may be able to put the shirt on a rack <u>after</u> someone else has hung the shirt.

Use **Same/Different Overlay and/or Same/Different Yes/No Overlay,** pages 79 & 80. Once this skill is mastered, use the **Types of Hangers Overlay,** page 90, for extended practice and communication. The **Hanging Clothes Discussion Picture**, page 91, can be displayed as a reminder of hanging procedures.

Review the types of hangers and what they are used for. Allow students to take turns demonstrating correct hanging with each type of hanger for practice. The **Types of Hangers Overlay,** page 90, will be useful with this activity.

Shoulder Pads?

Hanging sweaters or shirts with shoulder pads is very tricky and requires a great deal of practice. Ask parents and faculty to save any shoulder pads they remove from their clothing, or make your own from fabric and foam (check with the local home economics classes for volunteers).

Skill: *Hanging T-shirts with shoulder pads.*
Activity: Have students practice hanging the T-shirts with shoulder pads. (Pin or sew these pads into T-shirts to make enough for students to practice hanging the shoulder pads.) The pads must be centered on the hanger arm after the garment is centered on the hanger.

Go To The Source

If possible, visit a local retail store and ask for a tour of the stockroom. Be sure to ask in advance for demonstrations of:

- Correct hanging procedures
- How hangers are stored and collected

Ask if students can observe employees actually processing merchandise to see how the hanging is done and how fast they have to hang the clothing. If a trip outside the classroom is not possible, the next best thing is to have someone from the store come talk to your class and bring some examples if possible. Many of the large chains have a person who will do this type of educational program.

NOTE: If you invite someone in to speak to your class, be sure to explain clearly what you are interested in and why. Please don't just ask them to come tell your class what they do.

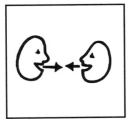

Vocabulary Words - Hanging Clothes

The 12 vocabulary words listed below are essential vocabulary words for hanging clothes in a retail store. Go over each word with the students. Use concrete objects and demonstrations to be sure the students can use the words or understand their use. After discussion, students can practice writing by copying the words.

hang	hanger	clothes
garment	size	straight
"foamies"	left	shoulder pads
stretch	neck	count

Worksheet - Vocabulary Words Practice

The **Vocabulary Practice Worksheet**, page 92, reinforces the vocabulary words. Cut out extra copies of the word blocks for students who cannot write and let them match the blocks onto their worksheet. Students who have the ability may write sentences or dictate sentences to each other.

Worksheet - Making Sentences With Vocabulary Words

Making sentences with vocabulary words. Use the worksheet, page 93, as a discussion page or seat work. It also makes a good homework sheet to help parents see what the student is learning. Students fill in the blanks with the words/symbols provided at the top of the page. They can write the word in or cut and paste the symbol. They could also draw a line from the symbol to the sentence it completes.

Worksheet 1
Hanger Selection

Name _____ Date _____

Directions: Draw a line from each piece of clothing to the correct type of hanger to use.

Teacher Directions: Using this worksheet, have the students draw a line to indicate the correct placement for each hanger. Some students may want to use a ruler with this. If desired, this worksheet can be laminated and a wipe-off pen used to make this activity resuable.

Worksheet 2
Hanger Selection

Name _____ Date _____

Directions: Draw a line from each piece of clothing to the correct type of hanger to use.

Teacher Directions: Using this worksheet, have the students draw a line to indicate the correct placement for each hanger. Some students may want to use a ruler with this. If desired, this worksheet can be laminated and a wipe-off pen used to make this activity resuable.

Retail Store Unit

Types of Hangers Overlay

blouse hanger

Women and Girls: blouses, dresses, skirts

foam hanger

Women and Girls: sweaters, large necks, materials that slide off hanger easily

children's hanger

Swimsuits and children's clothing

men's hanger

Men & Boys: shirts, light jackets

pants hanger

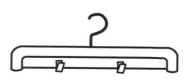

All Departments: pants, shorts, skirts

two-piece hanger

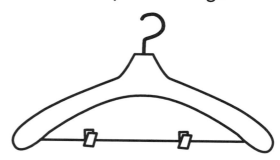

Sets: skirt and top, shorts and top, swimsuits

Teacher Directions: Use this page for classroom discussion and to help complete the Hanger Selection Worksheets 1 & 2. In addition, this overlay can be displayed in the classroom as a reminder of hanging procedures

Hanging Clothes Discussion Picture

Worksheet
Vocabulary Practice

Name _____ Date _____

These words are important to know if you work in a retail store. Talk about what each word means and then write them for practice.

hang	hanger	clothes
_____	_____	_____

garment	size	straight
_____	_____	_____

foamies	left	shoulder pads
_____	_____	_____

stretch	neck	count
_____	_____	_____

Worksheet
Making Sentences

Name _____ Date _____

Directions: Fill in the blanks in the sentences below with the correct word/symbol.

straight	hanger	left	match	pants hanger
|||	(hanger symbol)	←	◆ ◆	(pants hanger symbol)

1. A hanger with clips on it is probably a [ ] .

2. It is important to be sure clothing hangs [ ] on the hanger.

3. Shirts with no buttons must be hung by putting the [ ] through the bottom of the shirt so the neck does not get stretched.

4. In many stores, it is important to [ ] the size of the hanging garments.

5. A good rule is to have the "hook" of the hanger facing [ ] when putting the front of the garment on the hanger.

Teacher Directions: Make extra copies of the word blocks for students who cannot write and let them match the blocks to the question on the worksheet. Students who have the ability may write sentences or dictate sentences to each other.

Retail Store Unit

Packing & Unpacking Items

Retail Store: Objective 2

Student will demonstrate necessary skills to carefully unpack and repack items.

Overview

A large part of retail work involves receiving new merchandise, unpacking it, and preparing it for display on the "floor" (the retail portion of the store is referred to as the "floor"). Although most stores employ people to do primarily "receiving" or "stocking," all employees are called on at some time to help either unpack merchandise or prepare the merchandise for display when "the truck comes in."

Again, practice is essential so be sure that you have enough materials to keep the students busy for 45 minutes or more. Work should be done standing up. This is an excellent objective for partial participation for students who are physically unable to accomplish this task alone.

Suggested Activities

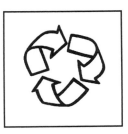

More Recycling!
Be sure to have enough work!
This objective will require practice and lots of material to practice with. For more ideas and suggestions, see the activity, **Recycle, Recycle, Recycle**, under **Retail Store Objective 1**, page 84. Items you will need to collect for the activities in this objective are:

■ Shoe boxes, cases shoe boxes came in, large packing cartons.

■ Old shoes to pack, small breakable junk items to practice safe packing (nonbreakable to start with).

Counting Items

Skill: *Counting items and writing the numbers down.*
Activity: During each of the activities in this objective, have students count the number of items completed and write it down: how many shirts they hung, how many cans they shelved, how many red shirts they hung, etc. *(See Counting Form, page 101, for an idea of how to have students record their work.)* This skill is essential in the retail business. The **Counting Overlay**, page 102, is designed to provide the students an opportunity to participate in the counting process.

But I Can't Count!

Skill: *Counting reinforcing techniques.*
Activity: If students can't count well or consistently, try counting five objects and marking the card, then doing five more and marking the card, etc. This can be a good technique even for students who can count if it becomes too time-consuming or awkward to count after the task is complete.

For students who cannot count at all, develop a "jig" for them to match to—a piece of cardboard with marks they can lay the item on, or a laminated 4x6 card they can "mark" as they finish an item, or use a chip or coin placed on a laminated card until the desired number of items is completed.

Worksheet — Counting Practice

After the students learn the concept of marking and counting, the **Counting Practice Worksheet,** page 103, will provide extra practice. If the student can't write, pair him/her with a student who can write down the correct number. The **Counting Overlay,** page 102, can be used with this activity.

Laundry Blues

Teach students to fold their own clothes in functional situations.

Skill: *Folding clothing.*
Activity: Have students fold their own laundry or school items and put on a shelf as if they were being displayed (gym clothes, kitchen or bathroom laundry).

Fold Them So They Look Nice

Have students take folded clothes (especially T-shirts, sweaters, shorts, slacks, jeans) out of a box and then put on shelves or tables neatly.

> **Skill**: *Removing items from a box and then stacking the items.*
> **Activity:** This task can be varied by having students match and stack by other variables: style, color, size, etc.
>
> There needs to be at least 24 items (2 dozen), or more if possible, to simulate this work task. If this task is difficult, begin with towels or washcloths. Team uniforms are also a good item to practice on. Some teachers have students do the uniform laundry and then fold and deliver. Food service labs and the cafeteria are also good sources for laundry to fold.

Students who need more of a challenge can be in charge of counting the items at the beginning and then again at the end of the session, and keeping track of the numbers of items processed. The **Yes/No overlay,** page 81, is a good way to start this activity. As students advance with this skill, try the **Display Overlay**, page 104, and the **Counting Overlay**, page 102.

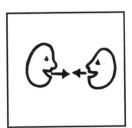

Vocabulary, Vocabulary, Vocabulary

The following are key vocabulary words for packing and unpacking.

same	more	help
count	fold	stack
box	trash	trash can
carry	price	hanger

Worksheet — Basic Vocabulary Practice

Use this worksheet, page 106, as a discussion starter or seat work. Students fill in the blanks with the words/symbols provided. This can be done as a small group activity or an independent activity depending on the ability level of the students.

Worksheet — More Vocabulary Words

Use this worksheet, page 107, to review some of the basic vocabulary words involved in retail work. The students are asked to match the pictures on the left with the words on the right. The worksheet itself is a basic matching worksheet, but it can serve as a good discussion and/or small group activity. It is also a good homework sheet to help parents see what the students are doing at school.

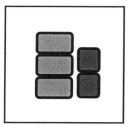

Don't They Look Nice

Skill: *Stacking like items together.*
Activity: When students are learning this skill, have them match to sample. For example, have one red shirt on the shelf and have them stack all the red shirts with it. The **Same/Different and Yes/No Overlay**, page 80, will be helpful in this activity. Next, have students sort to a picture of a red shirt or a red piece of paper on the shelf.

> **Key:** Remember that the key to making this activity a success is having enough work to simulate an actual job—45 minutes minimum.

At The Store

Anytime your class is in the community, point out displays of merchandise that are correct and also some that are sloppy or in a disarray. Make students aware of the concept of folding and displaying merchandise.

Skill: *Recognizing displays that are correctly and incorrectly done.*
Activity: Arrange for a store manager or other employee to demonstrate how they fold and display in various areas of the store.

If CBI trips aren't an option, try to get another high school student or former graduate to talk to your class about working in the receiving area and to demonstrate folding techniques.

"Cleaning" Shoes

The term "cleaning" shoes refers to the following steps:

■ Taking shoe boxes out of the carton they were shipped in.

■ Opening each shoe box and removing the packing paper.

■ Removing the shoes and cleaning out all the trash inside the shoe.

Shoes arrive at the store packed in shoe boxes and a great deal of trash paper, plastic, cardboard, sticks, etc. It is a very time-consuming job for employees to "clean" the shoes before displaying them.

Contact large discount stores and ask them to save shoe boxes for you. They are usually discarded since shoes are often displayed on shelves out of the boxes. Ask that they also save the case the shoes come in. You may have to explain why and be willing to pick boxes up that day since there is usually not storage in the receiving area of stores. Get old shoes from parents, faculty, and thrift stores. Be sure to include all sizes from baby shoes to adult shoes.

Skill: *Removing shoe boxes and packing materials from large boxes.*
Activity: Repack the shoes in the large packing cases so the students can practice unpacking and "cleaning" (stuff paper in the toes, wrap each shoe in newspaper, put in plastic bags, etc.) The **Yes/No and Same/Different Overlay**, page 80, will be helpful in this activity.

As students master the task of "cleaning," work with them on setting up their own work area, efficient work space, and safety awareness as they work. This is a boring job, but it is a job that many people do every day. Students need to learn to work at boring tasks too!

Repacking Shoes

In some stores, the shoes are "cleaned," and then put back into the shoe boxes for storage until they are displayed. As a rule of thumb, shoes are packed with soles to outside, toes at opposite ends. This is very difficult to do while shoes are tied together.

Skill: *Repacking shoes in boxes.*
Activity: Demonstrate to the students the proper way to fit a pair of shoes together "toe to heel, soles out." Then put each pair in its own box and put the lid on. Use the materials from the "cleaning shoes" activity described previously. Have the students be sure to stack the boxes neatly. Initial training can be done with shoes separate, and work up to doing the shoes tied together. Use a 10" string to tie the shoes together at the laces to simulate the way they are packed when new. Students needing additional challenge can use the counting procedures described in **But I Can't Count,** page 96, to keep track of their progress. At the end of each session, graphing the students' progress may serve as a motivator. Students can compete with one another, or try to better their "personal best." These students should be encouraged to maintain quality standards, however.

Worksheet — Matching Shoes to Shoe Box
Matching shoes to the correct box. Using the worksheet on page 105, have students draw a line to match the shoes and then the box they would go into. This worksheet can be laminated for reuse. The **Yes/No Overlay,** page 81 and the **Yes/No and Same/Different Overlay,** page 80, be helpful in this activity. Students can work independently, as a group, or pair students together.

How Do I Get It Open?

Most boxes arrive at the store with a great deal of tape and/or plastic binding around them so they do not come apart during shipping. Getting into these boxes is often a difficult and frustrating task. Box cutters are generally the easiest way to cut through the tape and/or binding, if safety is observed. This is a skill that should only be taught when there is close supervision since the blade in a box cutter is actually a razor blade.

Skill: *Use a box cutter to cut tape and open boxes.*
Activity: Discuss and demonstrate for the students safety guidelines for opening a box with a blade. Always cut away from your body to avoid injury. Scissors can be used if available. In the circumstance that there is not a sharp instrument available, a set of car keys will do. Again, always cut away from the body. Students should also be taught that if they cannot get a box open they have to ask for help.

Worksheet—Vocabulary Practice

Use this worksheet, page 108, as a discussion page or seat work. Students use the symbols at the top of the page to correctly complete the sentences below. Students can write in the word, draw a line, or use a symbol to complete the sentences. This is a good activity to pair writers and nonwriters.

Safety First

Use the **Safety Discussion Picture,** page 109, to help begin a discussion to review safe and unsafe practices when opening boxes and cartons.

Safety Discussion Picture

Skill: *Recognizing safety procedures.*
Activity: Have students brainstorm a list of rules for safe cutting procedures. Students can be put in groups to create safety posters illustrating the rules they came up with. Have each group present and explain the posters, and then display the posters in your classroom.

Counting Form

Name _____ Date _____

_____

Item Name or Stock #	Amount	Initials

Item Name or Stock #	Amount	Initials

Item Name or Stock #	Amount	Initials

Retail Store Unit

Counting Overlay

Worksheet
Counting Practice

Name _____ Date _____

Directions: Count the number of items. Make a mark for each item in the big box. Write the correct number in the small box.

Retail Store Unit

Display Overlay

fold	straighten the shelf
help	thank you
yes	no

Worksheet
Matching Shoes to Box

Name _____ Date _____

Directions: Draw a line from the shoe at the left to the shoe in the middle that matches it. Then connect them to the box that fits.

Worksheet
Basic Vocabulary Practice

Name _____ Date _____

Directions: Draw a line from the symbols to the correct word.

count

fold

same

trash

more

help

box

stack

same

more

help

count

fold

stack

box

trash

Worksheet
More Vocabulary Practice

Name _____ Date _____

Directions: Draw a line from the pictures on the left to the word on the right.

hanger

count

box

carry

trash can

fold

price

box

hanger

count

fold

price

trash can

carry

Worksheet
Vocabulary Practice

Name _____ **Date** _____

Directions: Fill in the blanks in the sentences below with the correct word/symbol.

scissors	shelf	count	key	trash	box

1. Folded clothes are often stacked on a table or [ ].

2. The best tool for opening a [ ] is a box cutter.

3. Two other ways to open a sealed box are [ ] and [ ].

4. "Cleaning" shoes means to take the [ ] out of the shoes to get them ready for display.

5. To find out how many shirts are in a box, you have to [ ].

Teacher Directions: Make extra copies of the word blocks for students who cannot write and let them match the blocks to the question on the worksheet. Students who have the ability may write sentences or dictate sentences to each other.

Safety Discussion Picture

Pricing Merchandise

> ## Retail Store: Objective 3
>
> *Student will demonstrate necessary skills
> to price merchandise.*

Overview

Pricing is a different process in each store. Notice carefully the next time you shop how many different ways there are to indicate the cost of an item:

- Large price labels that are attached by string or plastic.

- Small stick-on labels.

- Shelf prices.

- Signs above the items.

- A variety of other ways.

Large chain stores often do not price individual items (unless they are on sale), but use a shelf pricing system with shelf labels that match stock numbers of the items. Smaller stores are more likely to use price guns or price stickers. Attention to detail and eye-hand coordination are essential to this skill. It is also a process that is easily adapted for partial participation and cooperative work. It is important that prices are consistently labeled in the correct spot (usually top right of label) and that the product name is not obscured.

> Note: As with all suggested activities in this book, students are encouraged to work standing up. They should be provided with enough materials for at least 45 minutes of work.

Suggested Activities

General Retail Overlay

The General Retail Overlay is designed to allow students to communicate during the following activities. (If the **General Retail Overlay,** page 115, is overwhelming, use the **Yes/No Overlay,** page 81.) The concepts on this overlay are equally important for verbal and nonverbal students. Extensive practice with these concepts will be very helpful since all of the ideas on this overlay will generalize to almost any job situation.

Price Location

Locating the price on an item is the first step in learning to price.

> **Skill:** *Locating the price on a variety of items.*
> **Activity:** Bring in a variety of items with the price on the item and let students practice finding the price.

Worksheet — Pricing Location Practice

The **Pricing Location Practice Worksheet,** page 116, provides practice in locating various types of prices on items. This worksheet would be an excellent follow-up activity to a community experience of locating prices in a store.

Don't Shoot

Contact local stores to find a price gun to borrow. This may be difficult because stores don't like to let price guns leave the store. Often, employees must sign them in and out. They may, however, allow you to come to the store to learn how to use a price gun. This is an important skill and unfortunately very difficult to simulate. You may want to consider purchasing one or asking a business or club to donate one for you to use in vocational training.

> **Skill:** *Holding a price gun correctly.*
> **Activity:** If a price gun is not available, use the hand held label makers that are readily available in office supply stores—the motor skills are similar.

Getting the Right Squeeze

Skill: *Sticking labels on merchandise.*

Activity: *Developing prerequisite motor skills*: Use spray bottles to develop coordination. Use colored water to practice spraying into a specific area marked on a window or mirror (this skill is also used in laundry/housekeeping, page 263).

Pricing Can Be A Tacky Situation

Prices are often printed on labels that must be stuck on by hand. They must be placed in specific areas on most products. They cannot cover the brand name or other information that "faces" the public.

Skill: *Sticking labels on merchandise.*

Activity: Use any type of labels or stickers on a page or roll. Have students put one label on each item (soda cans, boxes, papers, envelopes, etc.).

If they cannot peel labels off independently, pull stickers off and stick onto edge of table so they can grab edge and stick onto the item. Cardboard can be folded to make an edge raised for easy grasping. This is a task that can be done by someone with very limited range of motion if the stickers are prepared so they can touch them. If stickers are too sticky, the students may want to apply a small amount of hand lotion.

Practice, Practice, Practice

Skill: *Practice sticking labels on merchandise.*

Activity: Save shampoo and detergent bottles for this practice. They are durable and can be used again and again. They can also be used for practicing facing skills in the Grocery Store Unit. Remember, you will need as many as possible to make a work task simulation - at least 24, but more would be better. Do this task standing up.

"X" Marks The Spot

Prices must be attached in specific places. This task will allow the students to learn to focus on a particular area—front of container, usually top right corner. If no containers are available for practice, use laminated sheets of paper with squares or labels drawn on the paper.

Skill: *Sticking labels on merchandise in specific places.*
Activity: Make a small 'X' on items to assist students in getting sticker/label in correct location.

HELPFUL HINT: Give students one item correctly priced/labeled so they will have a sample to match to and/or use the **Sticker Location Sample Sheet**, page 117, to give visual help in placing the stickers.

Worksheet — Sticker Placement Practice
This worksheet, page 118 provides an opportunity to review the previous activity on pricing. Have students mark where they would put the price sticker. Use actual containers in the shape of each picture for a concrete reference. As a group, go over each item, then allow the students to complete it independently or pair students.

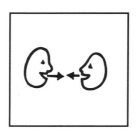

Vocabulary, Vocabulary, Vocabulary
The following are vocabulary words useful for the pricing objective.

bottom	store	price
stock number	front	

Worksheet - Vocabulary Words
The **Vocabulary Practice Worksheet,** page 119, is a vocabulary comprehension task. The student will match a word to the box that tells about the word.

General Retail Store Overlay

I'm finished.	please
I need help.	thank you
yes	no

Worksheet
Pricing Location Practice

Name _____ Date _____

Directions: Circle the price on each item or tag.

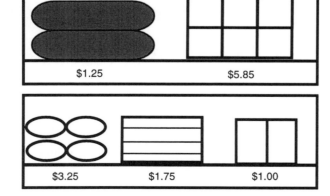

Sticker Location Sample Sheet

Retail Store Unit

Worksheet
Sticker Placement Practice

Name _____ Date _____

Directions: Put an "X" where the price sticker should go.

Vocabulary Practice

Name _____ Date _____

Directions: Match the pictures with the clues.

bottom	How much something costs.
store	The side of the product that should face the customer.
price	The side of the product that is not a good place for a price tag.
stock number 12345678	The number that tells what the product is and where it goes.
front	Where items are sold.

Retail Store Unit

Stocking Shelves

Retail Store: Objective 4

Student will demonstrate ability to stock shelves

Overview

The primary objective of retail stores is to sell merchandise. The managers want the shelves, tables, and hanging racks to be neat and organized. Sizes should be easy to find. It is not surprising that a great deal of time is spent stocking (or putting stock on shelves as it arrives and keeping the displays current). Almost every employee in a retail store from custodians to the manager is expected to assist with keeping the store appealing.

Endurance is a critical aspect of this job. Workers are expected to stay busy, standing if at all possible. Because employees usually stock without close supervision, self-initiation is very important. Encourage independence and problem solving. Student must learn to use good manners and treat customers with respect at all times.

Suggested Activities

Matching Color

Skill: *Matching colored items to same color on shelf.*
Activity: For initial instruction, solid objects should be used (cans covered with colored contact paper, boxes with colored labels, colored plastic cups and/or plates at least 20 of each color). Place one object on shelf and have student stock the shelves by color.

After initial instruction, use folded clothes (towels, washcloths, T-shirts, etc.) to practice this skill. (Handling folded clothes without unfolding them is a skill in itself.) Try to make color the most notable difference. Use the term "stocking" during this task. Use the **Same/Different Overlay,** page 79, to practice this activity.

Matching style

Skill: *Matching similar styles of clothing to each other.*
Activity: Begin with obvious discrimination tasks (T-shirts vs. button shirts) and progress to finer discrimination (button shirts with button-down collars vs. button shirts without button-down collars). This skill is easier to teach with clothes on hangers than with folded clothes—the differences are easier to see.

It is helpful if style is the most obvious variable. Other options for style choices are women's vs. men's, adults vs. children's, work clothes vs. dressy clothes. Whichever style you choose, it is important to have enough work to keep the students busy for at least 45 minute Use **Same /Different** and/or **Yes /No & Same /Different Overlay,** page 79 or 80.

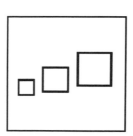

Matching Size

The concept of size in retail is a number and/or letter matching task rather than an actual size discrimination task. There are tags sewn in or on the garment to denote size and usually a tag attached with size and price information attached. Hanging sizes together is common: all the size 8 dresses hang together to make them easy for the customer to find.

Skill: *Sorting like-size items and placing them together.*
Activity: This activity involves the teacher pinning tags to clothes of any kind. (This can be an activity for students who have mastered this particular skill.) Tags can be cut out of cardboard (or copy and laminate the **Size Tag Activity 1,** page 127 and cut out). There should be at least 20 of each size. The more items the students have to work with, the more practice they have in the skill and in developing endurance. Mix all the clothing up in a box or have students randomly hang onto a rack. Have the students sort and re-hang on the rack according to size (use size "collars" on **Size Tag Activity 2,** page 128). If students are unable to match numbers, begin by using color coded tags and "collars."

Another twist to this activity would be to use **S, M, L,** and **XL** for sizes in the same manner. Once students have mastered this skill, let them pin (with safety pins) the correct size tag on clothes for other students to use.

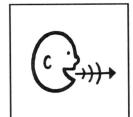

Communication Practice

Skill: *Recognizing and communicating when items do not match.*
Activity: Using the **Matching Overlay,** page 129, show students a pair of items used in one of the previous activities. Say to the student, "these two items match." If they do not match, the student should say "no" or a similar negative response or use the overlay section marked "wrong." Ask the students, "What is wrong with the match? Is it the size?, Is it the color?, Is it the style?" Use the **Matching Overlay,** page 129, to answer these questions if necessary.

Worksheet — Matching Styles

The **Matching Styles Worksheet,** page 130, offers an opportunity to practice the skills developed in the previous two activities. The students are to draw a line from each piece of clothing on the right to the matching style on the left side. This can be done as an independent activity or a group discussion. This is a good indication of how much more intensive practice the students will need to master this skill.

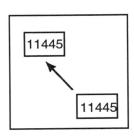

Matching Stock Numbers

Skill: *Match long stock numbers to each other.*
Activities: Make 10-20 copies of the **Stock Number Matching Activity,** page 131, laminate, and cut out the stock numbers. Copy one page and laminate without cutting. Mix up laminated cards and have students match to a single copy of the **Stock Number Matching Activity** page. If students are unable to match the long numbers, let them match/sort by the first digit or color code and sort by color.

Where Does This One Go?

Skill: *Matching stock numbers on shirt to stock numbers on shelves.*
Activity: Pin a piece of paper with a five- to ten-digit number on each shirter (or make 10 or more copies of the **Stock Number Matching Activity,** page 131). Make at least 24 tags, but more is better. Put file labels with the same numbers on them across a shelf. The students can then fold the shirts and match the "stock numbers" on the tag to the shelf. Use single digit numbers if necessary or color code the tickets for students who cannot match numbers. Most stock numbers are at least six digits long. Use the **Stocking Overlay,** page 132, for this activity.

Worksheet — Matching Stock Numbers

The **Matching Stock Numbers Worksheet,** page 133, provides an opportunity to practice matching stock numbers. There are two shelves on the page, each with three stock labels on them. Students should draw a line from each box to the place on the shelf that matches the stock number on the box.

Displaying Merchandise

Using the **Stocking Overlay,** page 132, review the concepts of same/different, yes/no, stock number, and the question, "Where does this one go?"

> **Skill:** *Recognizing misplaced and incorrectly placed items.*
> **Activity:** Using the materials from the previous activities (**Matching Size** and **Where Does This One Go?**), set up several displays in the classroom (on a shelf, on a table, on chairs, etc.) with some being correct and some incorrect: mismatch stock numbers, turn items in various directions so they are not all facing correctly, etc. Using the **Sample Display Questions,** page 134, ask the students questions about the displays.

This is a chance to extend communication in this area for both verbal and nonverbal students. For students who can read, the questions could be written so the students could carry them around to the different displays and answer the questions.

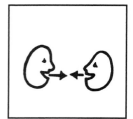

Beginning Vocabulary Words

This activity is designed to build the vocabulary words and phrases necessary to stock and restock shelves. The beginning vocabulary words are as follows:

stockroom	truck	inventory
shopback	department	loading dock

> **Skill:** *Recognizing basic stocking vocabulary words.*
> **Activity:** Review the basic vocabulary words used for stocking shelves. Teachers can talk about each word and then show how the word is written.

Worksheet — Stocking Vocabulary Words

After reviewing the words listed above, use the **Stocking Vocabulary Words Worksheet,** page 136, to practice recognizing and writing the words.

Worksheet — Vocabulary Practice

The **Vocabulary Practice Worksheet,** page 137, is a general comprehension worksheet. Students are to fill in the blanks with the words/symbols provided at the top of the page. This can be a group activity or an independent one. It is a good activity to pair students who can read with those who cannot.

Recovery/Shopback

In many stores, there is a procedure called recovery or "shopback" in which an employee takes a cart (or basket) through the store picking up misplaced items, then locating the correct place to return the item. This is a difficult task requiring practice. Some stores keep carts or boxes near the cashiers for items that customers returned or decided not to buy. This skill goes well with Objective 2 in the **Grocery Store Unit,** page 25, on facing (straightening) shelves. Use the **Shopback Overlay**, page 135, for this activity.

> **Skill:** *Find misplaced items and put them in the correct place.*
> **Activity:** Have students use a cart or a grocery "basket" to pick up items that are out of place (place objects around the room — books, pencils, work materials, coats, clothes, etc.) and have students replace these items in the correct place. Use the **Shopback Overlay**, page 135, for this activity.

Recovery/Shopback Game

You can make this a team event, with one team moving a certain number of items out of place and the other team having to locate the items. Use the **Shopback Overlay**, page 135, for this activity. The materials used in the **Grocery Store Unit,** page 25, for facing shelves will work very well with this activity.

Left-Right Scanning

Teach students to scan left to right on a shelf for items that do not belong. Use items from Objective 1 of the **Grocery Store Unit,** page 15. This is a difficult concept for many students, but it is essential to use an orderly scanning process to successfully recover and replace shopbacks. Use the **Directional Scanning Overlay**, page 138, to let students direct you in locating and/or replacing shopback items on a shelf in the classroom.

> **Skill:** *Locate and replace misplaced items.*
> **Activity:** Stock a shelf or an entire set of shelves. Place some items out of place. Using the **Scanning Overlay,** page 139, to direct students to out of place items. Then have students direct you and finally let them direct each other. This can be done in a game type format with individuals or teams.

Worksheet — Scanning Practice

This is an opportunity to reinforce and practice the left-to-right scan. Use the **Scanning Practice Worksheet,** page 140. There are five shelves on the page. Each one has more than one error on it. The student should mark the **first** error he/she sees as he/she scans across the shelf. Emphasize the left-to-right and top-to-bottom scan. This skill will be important in many jobs.

Delivery Person

Skill: *Delivering items to customers.*
Activity: Have students make deliveries around the school from a cart. Begin at low traffic times and progress to high traffic times. Focus on turning corners and being safe around people.

Use the **Delivery Overlay,** page 141, for this activity.

Obstacle Course

Skill: *Maneuvering cart through an obstacle course without knocking down items.*
Activity: Set up an obstacle course in the school parking lot or other smooth area—use empty boxes, traffic cones, chairs, etc. Don't make this a race—focus on safety. Give points for safe maneuvering and deduct points for hitting things or not looking for cars. Use raw eggs or cotton balls in the baskets to emphasize the need to be careful. Use the **Delivery Overlay,** page 141, for this activity.

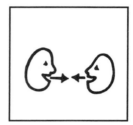

More Vocabulary Words

The major vocabulary words for stocking are as follows:

merchandise	shopback	stockroom
right	left	inventory
up	down	department
match	recycle	loading dock

Skill: *Recognizing stocking vocabulary words.*
Activity: Students can write, match, copy, and/or write sentences with the words. Use the **Vocabulary Practice Worksheet**, page 142, for this activity. It is an excellent opportunity to pair nonwriters with writers for cooperative work.

Worksheet — Vocabulary Matching

The **Vocabulary Matching Worksheet,** page 143, is another review of vocabulary. Students should match the symbols on the left side of the page with the vocabulary word it represents on the right side of the page. This is not intended to check comprehension, but to review the vocabulary.

Stocking Shelves Discussion Picture

Display **the Stocking Shelves Discussion Picture,** page 144, as a reminder of correct stocking procedure.

Size Tag Activity 1

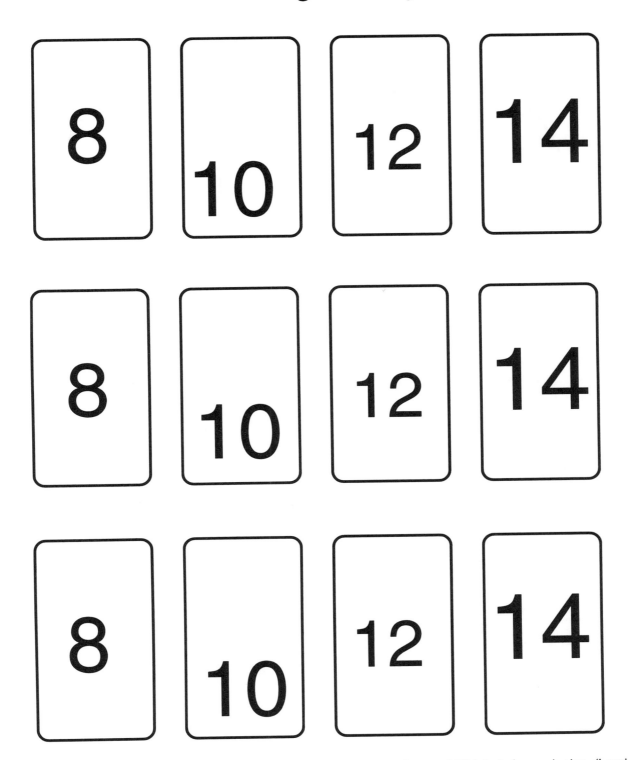

Teacher Directions: Make enough copies of this page to have a minimum of 20 labels for each size. (Laminate for durability.) Cut out each tag and pin (with safety pins) to items of clothing. Students can sort and hang up items by matching to like sizes.

Retail Store Unit

Size Tag Activity 2

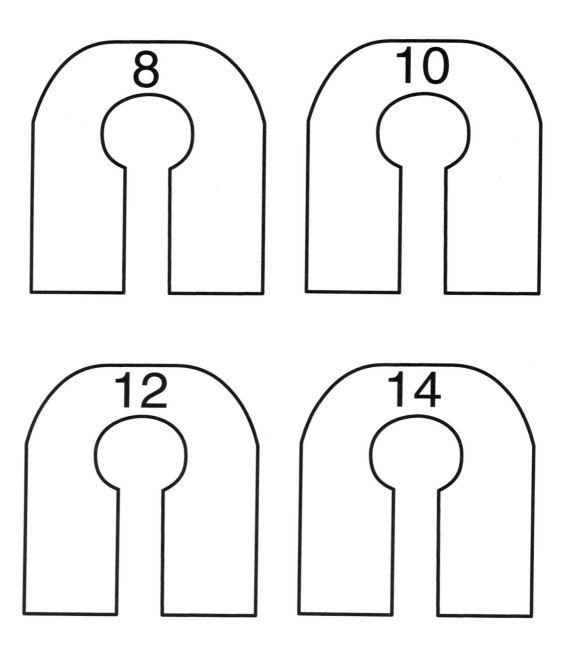

Teacher Directions: Copy, laminate, and cut out items on this page. Put size hangers on a rack and have students hang up items by matching correct sizes.

Matching Overlay

no

color

style

size

Retail Store Unit

Worksheet
Matching Styles of Clothes

Name _____ Date _____

Directions: There are three styles of clothes in the boxes in the middle. Match the remaining clothes to those three styles by drawing a line to the correct box.

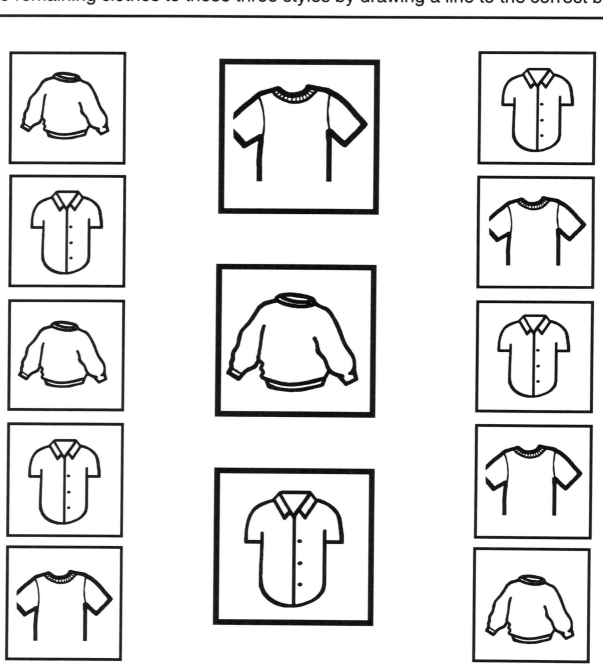

Stock Number Matching Activity

88011	**88017**
83793	**83795**
68837	**68838**
78067	**78060**
00086	**00088**

Teacher Directions: Make 10-20 copies of this page, laminate. Keep one sheet whole and cut out the stock numbers from the remaining copies. Mix up laminated cards and have students match individual stock numbers to numbers on the whole sheet.

Stocking Overlay

same	**different**
yes	**no**
stock number 68838	**Where does this one go?**

Worksheet
Matching Stock Numbers

Name _____ Date _____

Directions: Match the stock numbers on the boxes to the stock numbers on the two shelves. Draw a line from each box to the correct place on the shelf.

| 3245 | 4792 | 3248 |

3245   3248   3245   4792

4792   3248   3245

| 23451 | 23452 | 23453 |

23451   23453   23452   23451   23452   23453

23451   23453   23452   23451   23452

Sample Display Questions

Directions: Check each display in the room. Answer the questions under the same number.

Display #1

☐ Correct

☐ Incorrect

---- Needs to be faced.
---- Wrong stock number.
---- Sized wrong.
---- Colors are wrong.
---- Item out of place.

Display #2

☐ Correct

☐ Incorrect

---- Needs to be faced.
---- Wrong stock number.
---- Sized wrong.
---- Colors are wrong.
---- Item out of place.

Display #3

☐ Correct

☐ Incorrect

---- Needs to be faced.
---- Wrong stock number.
---- Sized wrong.
---- Colors are wrong.
---- Item out of place.

Display #4

☐ Correct

☐ Incorrect

---- Needs to be faced.
---- Wrong stock number.
---- Sized wrong.
---- Colors are wrong.
---- Item out of place.

Shopback Overlay

yes 	**no** 
I need help. 	**Where does this one go?** 
Do you have any shopbacks for me to take? 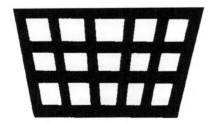	**I'm finished!** 

Worksheet
Stocking Vocabulary Words

Name _____ Date _____

Directions: These words are important to know if you work in a retail store. Talk about what each word means. Then write the word for practice.

stockroom _____	**truck** _____
inventory _____	**department** _____
shopback _____	**loading dock** _____

Worksheet
Vocabulary Practice

Name ——————————————— **Date** ———————

Directions: Fill in the blanks in the sentences below with the correct word or symbol.

I need help	I'm finished	please	left	Where does this one go?	Please write that down for me.

1. When you are doing shopbacks, start looking on the end of the shelf and go to the right end. ☐

2. If you don't know where an out-of-place item goes, you would say, ☐

3. If you can't find where an out-of-place item goes, you could say, ☐   Or ask: ☐

4. After you have put all shopbacks up correctly, tell your boss: ☐

5. You try to make a delivery to Mr. Jones. The person who comes to the door says, Mr. Jones is out today. To be sure you have the message correct you may ask: ☐

Teacher Directions: Make extra copies of the word blocks for students who cannot write and let them match the blocks to the question on the worksheet. Students who have the ability may write sentences or dictate sentences to each other.

Retail Store Unit

Directional Scanning Overlay

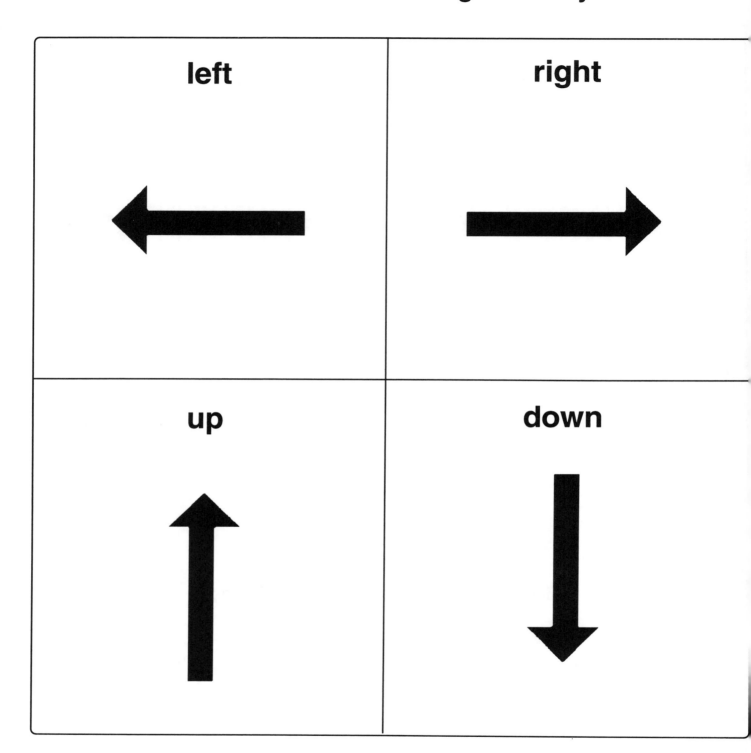

left

right

up

down

Scanning Overlay

Put it there.	yes	no
left	right	Please write that down for me.
up	down	There's one out of place.

Worksheet
Scanning Practice

Name _____ Date _____

Directions: Start at the left of each row (shelf) and scan across to the right. Mark the first item that is out of place.

Delivery Overlay

hello	yes	no
thank you	I have a delivery.	Please write that down for me.
please	I need help.	Have a nice day.

Worksheet
Vocabulary Practice

Name _____ Date _____

Directions: These words are important to know if you work in a retail store. Talk about what each word means. Write them for practice.

merchandise	shopback	stockroom
_____	_____	_____

right	left	inventory
_____	_____	_____

up	down	department
_____	_____	_____

match	recycle	loading dock
_____	_____	_____

Worksheet
Vocabulary Matching

Name _____ Date _____

Directions: Draw a line from the symbol to the correct word.

	same
	different
	stock number
	I need help.
	I have a delivery.
	Would you please write that down.
	Put it there.
	Have a nice day.

Stocking Shelves Discussion Picture

Trash Disposal

Retail Store: Objective 5
Student will demonstrate appropriate trash disposal skills.

Overview

Almost all work in retail stores will generate trash. Trash often creates a safety hazard, especially for those with mobility challenges, and managers really dislike a messy customer area. Workers need to learn:

- To dispose of trash properly.
- To be aware when trash receptacles need emptying.

Trash can liners cost businesses money, so they do not want them wasted. Students should be taught and have ample opportunity to practice deciding if a trash can or box is full enough to empty. For many retail workers, the trash compactor is another aspect of proper trash disposal. Skills that involve decision making are often difficult to learn and require on going practice. This unit is meant to be a starting point to **begin** this skill learning process.

Suggested Activities

Keeping Work Area Free Of Trash
Have the students develop a habit of looking around their work area and picking up any trash. Keeping the work area free of trash is a safety skill as well as a customer relations skill.

Skill: *Keeping area free of trash.*
Activity: Set up situations where the students must go into a messy area to work. Cleaning up the work area before, during, and after work should become second nature over time. If a trash can is not available in the work area, teach the students to look for other options such as large boxes, store carts, trash bags, etc.

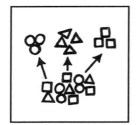

Sorting Trash: Cardboard, Plastic, Paper, Etc.

Students must also learn to distinguish between cardboard and other types of trash. Some stores use a recycling program where only cardboard can be placed in designated bins. Ask local retail stores to save cardboard out of shirts, shoes, or other small pieces, and also ask them to save the plastic they pull off packed merchandise. (If these sources are not available, cut up cardboard boxes into smaller pieces.)

Skill: *Recognizing and sorting different types of trash.*
Activity: Mix these pieces of cardboard in a large box or bin with pieces of wax paper, plain paper, envelopes, empty candy wrappers, and pieces of cellophane paper. Have students sort cardboard and noncardboard into appropriately marked boxes or bins. Begin with very easy discrimination such as cardboard and plastic; gradually increase discrimination tasks to include more variety and finer discrimination tasks. Use the **Sorting Trash Overlay**, page 150, for this activity and any time this skill is involved in the task at hand. *HINT: Save boxes from lunchroom, office, or ask local package stores to save them for you.*

Worksheet — Trash Sorting Practice

The **Trash Sorting Worksheet,** page 151, is a good review of the previous activity of sorting trash. It can be used as a group activity using real objects for demonstration and practice or as a follow-up independent activity. The students are to draw a line from the pieces/types of trash at the bottom of the worksheet to the correct dumpsite at the top of the page. The **Sorting Trash Overlay,** page 150, is useful with this activity.

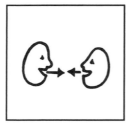

Vocabulary, Vocabulary, Vocabulary

The following are the vocabulary words used for sorting trash:

cardboard	retail store	trash
boxes	compactor	break down
clean up	safety	trash can
empty trash	trash bag	compactor
sort		

Show examples of these words and/or how the words are used. Use the **Trash Vocabulary Words Worksheet,** page 152, for this activity.

Worksheet — Vocabulary Practice
Use the **Vocabulary Matching Worksheet**, page 153. After reviewing the vocabulary words, students can draw a line from the symbols on the left to the words on the right. This is a good group activity or a good activity to pair readers and nonreaders. Students who can read the words can write sentences for practice.

Breaking Down Boxes
Teach students to "break down" or flatten boxes. This is an essential skill in business where they use a trash compactor.

> **Skill:** *Removing tape and wire and flattening cardboard boxes.*
> **Activity:** To "break down" a box, the ends need to be pulled or pushed out so the box will lie flat. Usually the tape or sealing wire must be removed.

This is a good time to teach students to ask for help if they cannot accomplish this task alone. It should become a habit to automatically break down a box when finished with it.

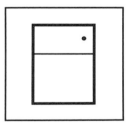

Using Trash Compactor
Many stores use trash compactors for their boxes since they do not have storage space in receiving areas. Most stores do not allow people under the age of 18 to operate compactors due to safety issues. Check with local stores and find several that use trash compactors. Have an employee demonstrate its safe use and discuss safety rules and potential hazards. This is not a skill that can be practiced in the classroom, but the safety issues can be discussed and reinforced.

Talk to the stockroom (often called "receiving") manager at a local retail store to see if they have any extra or old safety posters on safe use of a compactor (these items are updated often to keep the employee's attention on the safety issues). Find out who the representative is for the compactor company and contact that person for information and/or safety materials.

Does It Need To Be Emptied?
Students need to learn to check the trash can to see if it is empty. They should not automatically empty the can.

> **Skill:** *Recognizing when a trash can needs to be emptied*
> **Activity:** Set up situations where the student must decide whether the can needs emptying or not; e.g., one drink can—you should not empty the trash can; full of paper—you would empty the trash can.

Does It Need To Be Emptied? (continuted)

The **Full/Not Full Overlay,** page 155, is a good communication overlay to use while training. After the basic concept is mastered, switch to the **Empty Trash Overlay,** page 156, that deals more specifically with the task of emptying the trash.

Worksheet — Emptying The Trash

The **Emptying The Trash Worksheet**, page 154, deals with the decision making required to determine if an entire trash can needs emptying or not. There are seven trash cans and a picture of their contents. Students are to mark an "**X**" on the cans that need to be emptied.

Transferring Trash

Skill: *Transferring trash from container to container without spilling contents.*

Activity: Fill small bathroom-size trashcans or small boxes with trash and teach the students to transfer this trash to a larger can. Begin with trash cans filled with only paper and progress to cans filled with a variety of trash that is not as easy to transfer without making a mess. The **Full/Not Full Overlay,** page 155, and the **Emptying Trash Overlay,** page 156, are appropriate and helpful in this activity.

Trash Can Liners

Students need to learn to put trash bag liners in the cans.

Skill: *Putting trash bag liners in trash cans.*

Activity: Practice placing plastic trash liners in trash cans and removing the liner and securing the top for disposal. Often, businesses use trash bags that are too large for the cans and they must be tied around the top to stay up. Also, trash bags should be tied when they are removed from the trash can to avoid spills and/or accidents. This can be a very difficult task if the bag is too full. If the student is not physically able to tie the bag, then he/she must learn to ask for help when it needs to be done.

Use the **Empty Trash Overlay,** page 156, for students who need to ask for assistance. The ability to ask for assistance for any part of a task that a student cannot complete alone is essential for the maximum independent functioning. These needs may vary from specific site to specific site, but the general concept of asking others to help instead of waiting on someone to come to your rescue should be instilled as early as possible.

Real Life Practice

Have students empty trash cans in various classrooms, offices, or lounges. The **Practice Emptying Trash Overlay,** page 157, can be used to allow students to work more independently.

Sorting Trash Overlay

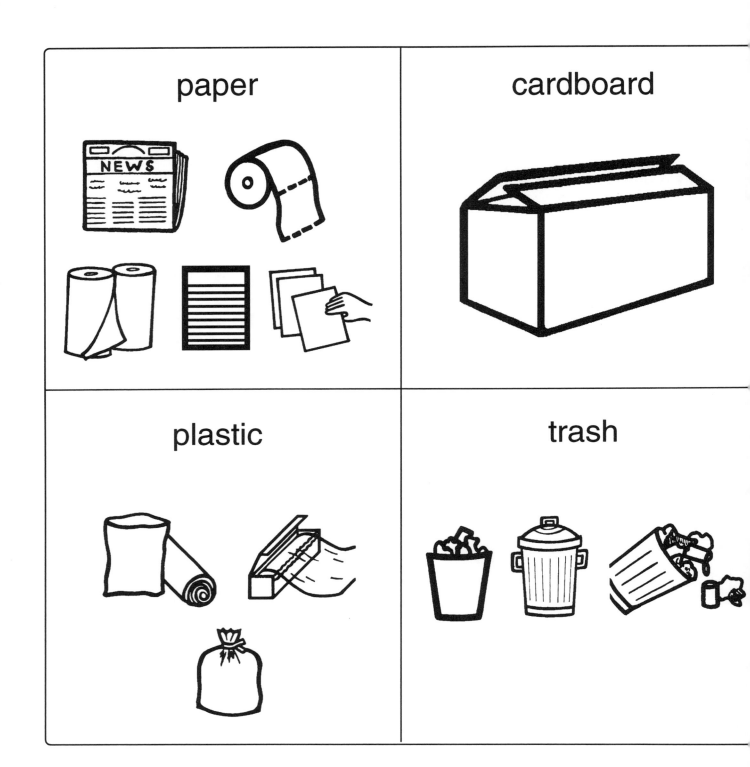

paper

cardboard

plastic

trash

Worksheet
Trash Sorting Practice

Name _____ Date _____

Directions: Draw a line from each piece of trash to the correct trash bin.

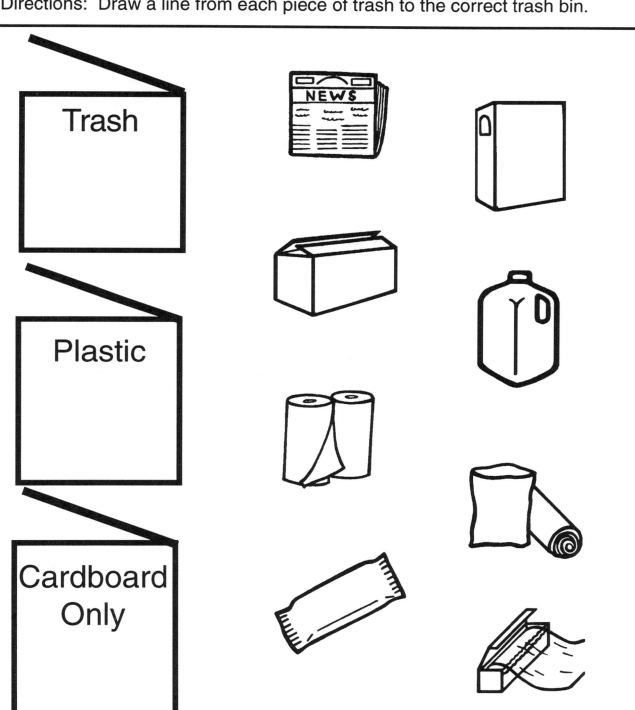

Retail Store Unit

Worksheet
Trash Vocabulary Words

Name _____ Date _____

Directions: These words are important to know if you work in a retail store. Talk about what each word means. Then write the word for practice.

___

cardboard

_____

retail store

_____

trash

_____

boxes

_____

compactor

_____

break down

_____

clean up

_____

safety

_____

Worksheet
Vocabulary Matching

Name _____ Date _____

Directions: Draw a line from the symbol to the correct word.

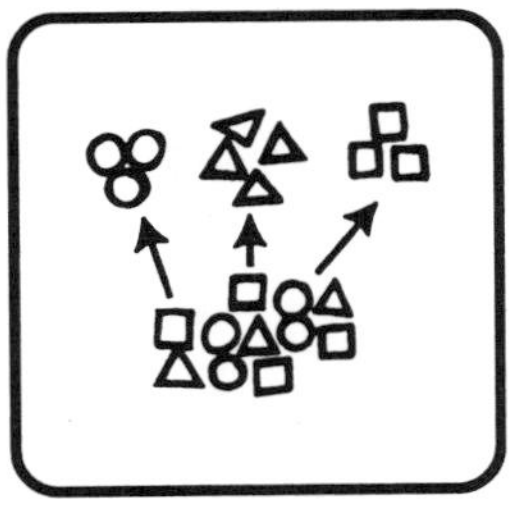

trash can

empty trash

trash bag

cardboard

compactor

sort

Worksheet
Is it time to empty the trash?

Name _____ Date _____

Directions: Put an "**X**" on the trash cans that need to be emptied.

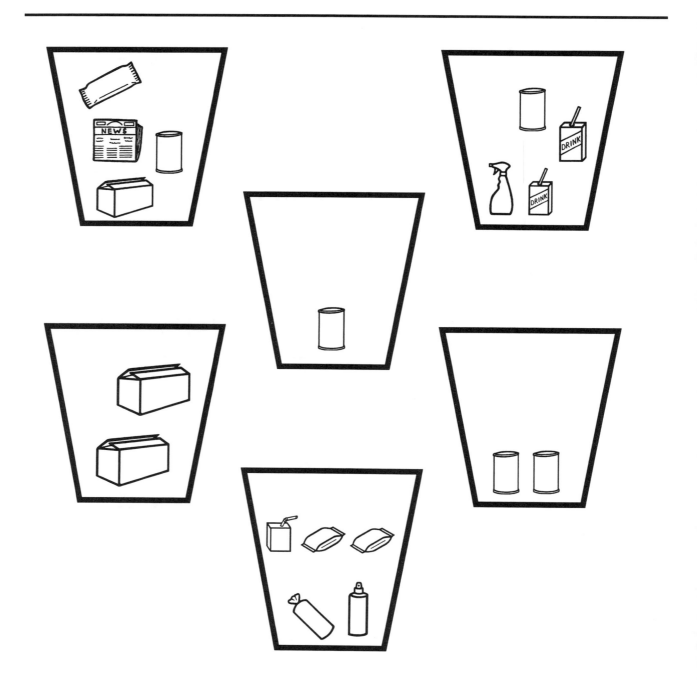

Full/Not Full Overlay

full

***not*
full**

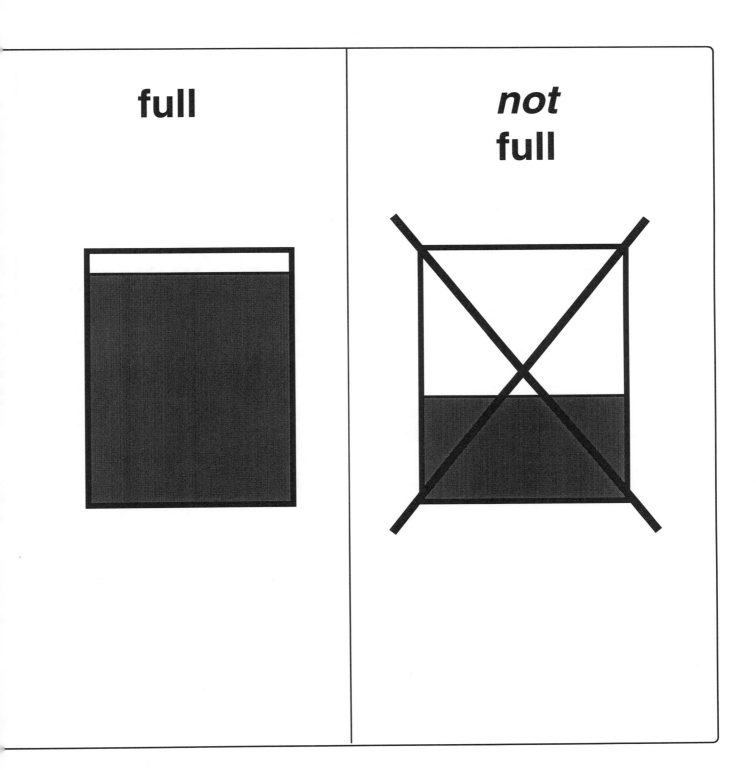

Empty Trash Overlay

Please help me. 	thank you 
This trash needs to be emptied. 	I'm finished. 

Practice Emptying Trash Overlay

hello	yes	no
thank you	Does your trash need to be emptied?	Please write that down for me.
please	I need help.	Have a nice day.

Carrying and Lifting

Retail Store: Objective 5
Student will demonstrate safe carrying and lifting practices.

Overview

It is the nature of retail sales that merchandise:

- Arrives in boxes.
- Must be stored.
- Must be transferred to the sales floor.

Boxes are sometimes moved by fork lifts or other mechanical devices. They are usually moved by hand. An employee looks for a specific stock number and takes that box to another area. There is a great deal of lifting, stacking, and moving of boxes. Matching to sample is a critical skill.

Incorrect lifting is one of the major causes of injury on the job. This concept must be reviewed often. Students rarely ask themselves if a box is too heavy to lift. These activities are designed to teach safe lifting strategies and provide opportunities for practice. Emphasize safety at all times.

Suggested Activities

Posters
Display safety posters. Most major retail stores have safety posters displayed in their break or sign-in area. Try to get the store to let your class see these or obtain copies for classroom use. Stores update these often to keep employee's attention focused on safety. They will often give you the old ones if you ask ahead of time.

Ask the Experts

Chiropractors usually have pamphlets on safe lifting. Ask a local chiropractor to show your class how to lift safely and what can happen to your spine/back if you don't. They usually have models of the spine to help demonstrate the danger of unsafe lifting. Don't forget the physical therapist and/or school nurse as resources for this information. It cannot be repeated too often. Talk with the janitor/custodian/maintenance staff in your school and find out where they post the safety information on lifting.

Practice, Practice, Practice

Skill: *Practice lifting using safe-lifting techniques.*
Activity: Have the students practice moving boxes so it becomes routine. Be sure they practice using the proper lifting techniques (bent knees, straight back, lift with thigh muscles). This can be tied to routine cleaning activities.

Always practice correct lifting techniques and comment to students when they use the proper techniques. This cannot be practiced enough. The **Moving Stock Overlay,** page 164, can be introduced at this time. Students need to learn to ask for assistance if they are going to handle boxes because two people are often required for safe lifting.

Two Person Lift

Use the **Moving Stock Overlay,** page 164, to begin a discussion about what a two person lift is. Talk to students about the fact that both persons lifting must talk to each other and communicate about timing for the lift. They also must practice safe lifting (bent knees, straight back, lift with thigh muscles) even though there are two people lifting.

Skill: *Lifting boxes with another person using safe lifting techniques.*
Activity: Use **Role Playing Retail Store 1,** pages 165 & 166, to help in your discussion of this topic. Let the group read, listen to or watch the role play activity and then discuss the outcome. The **Moving Stock Overlay,** page 164, can be helpful with this activity. Use the **Safe Lifting Discussion Picture**, page 167, to remind students of the importance of safe lifting.

Safe Lifting Discussion Picture

Picture Perfect

Take photos of students doing correct and incorrect lifts (knees bent, back straight, two people for heavy lifting, wearing a back support belt). Emphasize use of back support belts. Use the photos to make a safety wall display.

Black Belts - OSHA Regulations

Anytime lifting involves 20 pounds or more, a safety back belt is required for lift support. Most stores issue back belts as standard equipment for receiving and/or stock personnel. The custodian or vocational teachers in your school should have these. Have them demonstrate correct use. Students either really like wearing them, or won't wear them because they don't look "cool." Make wearing a safety belt a requirement for any lifting in the classroom.

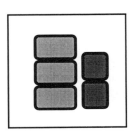

Stacking Boxes Safely

This is another skill that cannot be practiced enough. It should become second nature.

Skill: *Stacking boxes on top of each other in a correct manner.*
Activity: Using boxes of various sizes, demonstrate for students what happens if boxes are stacked incorrectly: large boxes on top of small boxes, boxes not balanced securely on a stack, boxes stacked too high, stacks that lean, etc.

Role Plays and Practice

Let students take turns correctly stacking boxes. Other students can judge whether they are correct or not. Always point out what the problem is. Having boxes fall everywhere often makes more of an impression than talking.

Skill: *Practice stacking boxes and recognizing when they are stacked incorrectly.*
Activity: Practice stacking boxes of all sizes. Use **Role Play Activities 1 & 2,** pages 165-166, to review and practice this concept. This can be done as a group activity or made into a team game. Assign students a "character" in the role play script. Help them read and act out the parts (reading is not essential with adult assistance.) Discuss the situations and alternatives/consequences of the choices. Let students create their own role plays for each other once they learn how to do them.

Video taping is a fun activity to combine with role plays and makes an excellent forum for review.

Retail Store Unit

Worksheet—Stacking Boxes Correctly

This worksheet is a review of the previous activities of safe lifting and stacking of boxes. Students are asked to put an "X" on boxes that are stacked incorrectly. Use real boxes and demonstrate what could happen with the incorrectly stacked boxes.

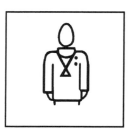

More Ask The Experts

Ask the manager of a large retail store, especially discount stores, if he will give your class a tour of the stockroom and talk about safety in that area. Be prepared that some stores are very sensitive about the general public seeing these storage areas. However, stores are generally proud of their safety programs and are willing to talk about them and share their successes.

Locating Boxes Using Stock Numbers

Employees must often locate a specific box. The most common way this is done is to look for specific stock numbers—either from an invoice or a list.

Skill: *Matching stock numbers.*
Activity: Make two copies of **Stock Number Activity Page 1**, page 169, and cut into individual tags and tape to boxes in the classroom or in a storage closet. Make another copy of the **Stock Number Activity Page 1**, laminate, and cut out the individual tags. Begin by giving the student one laminated tag to locate the matching box. As students master this basic skill, give them two to three tags. (This is an excellent opportunity to reinforce safe lifting and stacking skills.)

When the above activity is mastered, give students a printed/typed list of two or more stock numbers to locate see **Stock Number Activity Page 2,** page 170. The next step would be to hand-write a list of stock numbers for them to find.

Hint: Boxes don't have to be large cases. Save cereal boxes or other similar kitchen boxes (laundry detergent, oatmeal canisters, etc.).

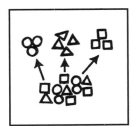

Sorting And Stacking Using Stock Numbers

Using the materials from the previous activity, set up several areas for students to "stock."

Skill: *Stocking shelves and matching stock numbers to shelf number.*
Activity: Make a copy of **Stock Number Activity Page 2,** page 169. Cut out the tags and attach them to shelves and/or tables so students can match the boxes to the correct shelf. Use this activity to review and emphasize left-right scanning. If this task is too difficult, try one or more of the following:

Reduce the number of digits on the tags.

Color code the tags.

Pair students for this activity.

This is a great opportunity to practice asking for assistance.

Worksheet—Invoice Number Matching

The **Invoice Matching Worksheet,** page 171, worksheet is designed to provide additional practice matching stock numbers on boxes to invoices. There are three numbered invoices on the left. Students are to match the boxes to the right to the correct invoice and mark an "X" on any box not on the invoice. This same activity can be done with actual boxes.

Worksheet—Label Matching

The **Label Matching Worksheet,** page 172, provides additional practice in matching numbers with different fonts. This is often difficult for students since the numbers on the invoice are often computer generated and hard to read while the numbers on the boxes may be handwritten or otherwise marked.

Situation Cards

Use the situation cards, pages 174-177, as group discussion starters. The **Situation Card Overlay,** page 173, can help with these discussions.

Moving Stock Overlay

Please help me.

thank you

Do you need help?

This is heavy.

Role Play: Retail Store I

Jack and Nick work together in a retail store. They work in the stockroom. Jack is working in his area, moving boxes from one place to another. Nick comes over to check on his friend.

Nick: "Hey, Jack, that's a pretty big box. You better let me help you."

Jack: *Bragging* "Nah, I've lifted boxes lots bigger than this. I bet you five dollars I can lift it."

Nick: "No, man, wait. . .Jack, stop. Let me help you."
(Jack picks up the box and gets it pretty high up, but it is too heavy and crashes to the floor. There is a sound of breaking glass, then silence.)

Jack: "What was in that box, man?"
(The manager comes over to check on the noise.)

Manager: "Let's check on the front of the box. . .Oh, no. . .That was a color T.V. Jack, next time you need to get someone to help you with a heavy box like that. Clean this up. Then come see me in my office."

Nick: "Guess you lost your bet, man."

Questions:

1. What should Jack have done? What is a two-man lift?

2. What do you think might happen to Jack now?

3. If you were Jack, what would you say to the manager?

Role Play: Retail Store II

Elizabeth and Kathy work in the stockroom of the retail store. They have just seen a training video of work safety. This video was about safe work habits in the stockroom. Robby and Chad are unloading boxes from a delivery truck.

Elizabeth: "Hi, guys! You sure have a lot of work."

Robby: "Yeah! That truck was packed! We have enough to keep us busy for a while."

Kathy: "Hey Chad. Don't you think you should be more careful about stacking those boxes?"

Chad: "Umm. . . No. I mean, I guess they'll be OK. It's just that we've got so many boxes and our break is in 30 minutes."

Robby: "Yeah, they'll be fine. Just put this one anywhere, Chad. I want to get to the breakroom before all the candy bars are sold out."

Elizabeth: "No, really guys. You should be more careful. Haven't you seen the safety video? It talks about stacking boxes the right way. You have to build a good foundation and put the little ones on top. Your stack looks pretty wobbly!"

Chad: "Get real, Elizabeth. We know what we're doing. Besides, if we take too much time, we'll miss our break. And the guys who come in after us can always straighten up these stacks if they don't like them."

Kathy: "How would you like it if somebody left a big mess like this to clean up?"

Elizabeth: "Look out, Robby that big box is headed your way. You guys shouldn't have put it on top of that little one. It's falling!" (A big box falls from the top of the stack, knocks down Robby, and lands on his ankle.)

Robby: "OOOWWW! Somebody get this box off of me. I think this stupid box broke my ankle!" *(Chad, Kathy and Elizabeth rush to help Robby.)*

Elizabeth: "Well, Robby, it looks like you'll be taking your break in the Emergency Room. I wonder if they have candy bars there?"

Questions:

1. What should the boys have done?

2. Why is it important to stack boxes safely?

3. How would you feel if you were in charge of cleaning up all the fallen boxes while Robby is in the Emergency Room?

4. Think of some reasons why it is not good to be unsafe at work.

Lifting/Stacking Discussion Picture

Worksheet
Stacking Boxes Safely

Name _____ Date _____

Directions: Put an "X" on the boxes that are not stacked safely.

Stock Number Activity Page 1

88011	**88017**
83793	**83795**
68837	**68838**
78067	**78060**
00086	**00088**

Stock Number Activity Page 2

Invoice 123	**Invoice 423**	**Invoice 723**
88011	68838	00088
68837	78060	68837

Invoice 223	**Invoice 523**	**Invoice 823**
78067	83793	00086
00088	88017	68837
68838	78060	78060
83795		

Invoice 323	**Invoice 623**	**Invoice 923**
83793	68837	88011
78067	88011	83795
00086	78060	68837
88017	00088	778060

Worksheet
Invoice Numbers Match

Name _____ Date _____

Directions: Draw a line from each box to the correct invoice by matching the stock number on each box to the invoice numbers. Put an "X" on boxes that are not on the invoices.

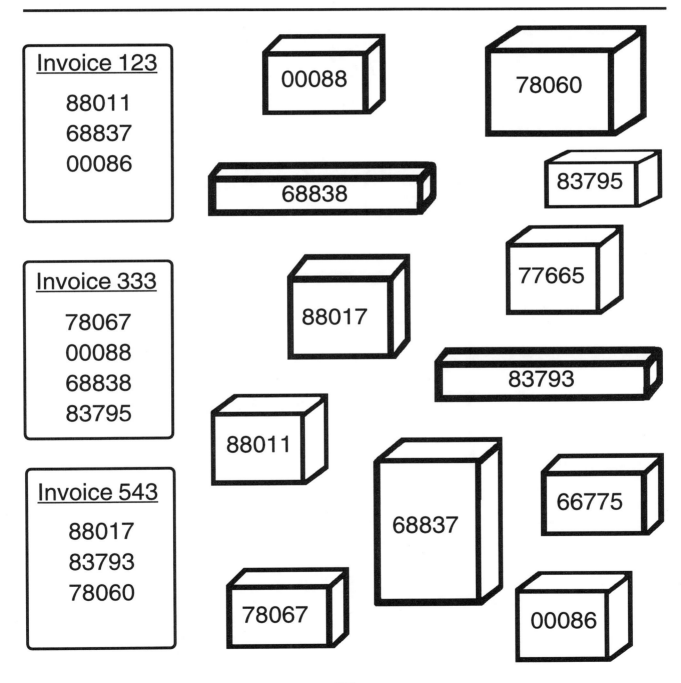

Invoice 123
88011
68837
00086

Invoice 333
78067
00088
68838
83795

Invoice 543
88017
83793
78060

00088
78060
68838
83795
77665
88017
83793
88011
66775
68837
78067
00086

Retail Store Unit

Worksheet
Matching Labels

Name _____ Date _____

Directions: Draw a line from each stock label to the correct label at the top of the page.

| 1234 | 7891 | 6543 |

1234   **7891**

7891   **6543**   **1234**

7891   *6543*

6543   **7891**   1234

1234   6543

Situation Card Overlay

Retail Store Unit

Retail Situation Cards

Juan is working in a stockroom. He is opening big cartons that are filled with bottles of shampoo. He takes the bottles out of the carton puts a price tag on them, and packs them back in the carton, ready to take out to the shelves. He has been working on this all morning. Halfway through his fourth carton, he realizes that the price tags he was using are all wrong. They are for bug spray that is $2.00 more!

What should Juan Do?

1. Put his cartons in Pablo's work space so Pablo can get the blame.

2. Leave the bottles with the wrong tags. Maybe no one will notice.

3. Let his supervisor know that he will be reticketing this merchandise right away.

DeDe is hanging up some beautiful shirts. She likes to do this—it is easy for her and she enjoys seeing the pretty new styles. Her supervisor stops by with a big carton full of shoes. He tells DeDe that he needs them right away for a sale display. DeDe hates to work with shoes. Pulling off the plastic hurts her fingers and sometimes they are stuffed with tissue paper that is hard to take out.

DeDe should:

1. Ask someone else to work on the shoes.

2. Stop what she is doing and begin on the shoes right away—the manager has a good reason for asking her to do this job.

3. Ignore the manager and continue to hang the shirts.

Retail Situation Cards

Annabel is putting price tags on merchandise on the floor of the store where she works. This means that instead of working back in the stockroom, she is working out where the customers are. She enjoys the work because she likes to work where she can hear the music. But a customer comes up to Annabel with a question, "Where can I find the sweaters?" Annabel does not know.

Annabel should:

1. Stop her work and find someone to help the customer.

2. Ignore the customer and continue with her work, hoping the customer will go away.

3. Say, "I don't know." Then keep her eyes on her task, and not look at the customer.

Jesse works unloading trucks on the loading dock of a big store. He has been bored all day because the truck he is supposed to unload is not at the store. It is stuck in traffic. Finally it comes, but it comes 10 minutes before Jesse's break is scheduled.

Jesse should:

1. Work unloading the truck for exactly 10 minutes, then take his break as scheduled.

2. Not even bother to start unloading the truck because there wouldn't be enough time to get it done before his break.

3. Start to work right away and unload the truck until it is empty because he had enough of a break while waiting for the truck to come.

Retail Situation Cards

Miranda has a job that she loves at the local department store. She also has a new boyfriend. Her boyfriend, Spike, has started calling her at work. At first they just talked during her breaks, but now Spike has begun to call her at all times. Several times a day, she has to stop working to talk to Spike. The manager has called Miranda into the office and warned her that the phone in the break room is only for emergency personal calls.

What should Miranda do:

1. Quit her job so she has more time to talk to Spike.

2. Tell Spike that she can only talk to him on the phone when she is home.

3. Nothing, just keep talking to Spike and hope that she doesn't get fired.

Tanya has just begun a new job at a department store. The manager asked her to work in the stockroom hanging up clothing that comes out of boxes. Tanya opens the first box in a big room full of boxes. It is full of beautiful sweaters in all colors. Tanya looks through the box and finds a sweater in her size. It would be perfect to wear on her date with her new boyfriend tonight. She decides she must buy it, and luckily she has money in her purse.

Tanya should:

1. Stop immediately, go find her purse and buy the sweater.

2. Finish her work and buy the sweater after work is over.

3. Hide the sweater in her locker and take it home without paying for it.

Retail Situation Cards

Bill has just started working at a hardware store. He is using a pricing gun to put prices on cans of paint. He finishes pricing all the cans, then realizes that he does not know what to do next.

Bill should:

1. Find the manager and ask.

2. Go on break; there's probably not any more work to do.

3. Put the cans out where he thinks they might go.

Laundry/ Housekeeping Unit

Laundry/Housekeeping Unit

The hospitality and service industry is one of the major employment opportunities in the current job market. As Americans gain more disposable income and more leisure time, there is a greater need for workers in the areas of laundry and housekeeping. In this unit, students are introduced to some basic skills necessary for success in this industry. These include:

- Sorting
- Folding
- Following directions
- General cleaning skills

Support materials for this unit include a variety of communication overlays specific to these tasks, worksheets on several levels, data collection and assessment forms, as well as a listing of vocabulary words and related concepts. Also included are forms designed to foster communication between school and home. Objectives for this unit include:

Objective 1: *Systematic cleaning skills (page 193).*
Objective 2: *Sorting, folding, and stacking laundry (page 207).*
Objective 3: *General cleaning skills (page 223).*
Objective 4a: *Office/public area cleaning (page 245).*
Objective 4b *Bedroom cleaning skills (page 255).*
Objective 4c: *Bathroom cleaning skills (page 265).*
Objective 4d: *General room cleaning skills (page 283).*

There are standard forms and overlays that are used for each unit. These include:

Vocational Update Letter to Parents — Use this form to send home with the student before the unit objective begins. It will give the parent or caregiver an overview of the unit objective plus extend the activity into the home (see page 182).

Calendar of Skills — Home activities that help reinforce skills learned in school (see page 183).

Vocabulary Words — Common vocabulary words used throughout the four objectives (see page 184).

Evaluation/Documentation Forms — Use these forms to assess goal achievement and/or formulate IEP goals and objectives (see pages 185-188).

Clean/Dirty Overlay — Simple overlay used with many of the unit objectives (see page 189).

Clean/Dirty and Yes/No Overlay — A four-choice overlay used with many of the unit objectives (see page 190).

Yes/No Overlay - A two-choice overlay used with several of the unit objectives (see page 191).

Vocational Update

Dear Parents,

In class, we are working on a unit to learn skills important to laundry/housekeeping jobs.

These are some vocabulary words we are using:

These are some activities you might want to try at home:

Thank you for your support in this important learning experience. Please sign and return.

Very truly yours,

_____

Parent signature _____

Calendar of Skills

☐ Talk about clean and dirty clothes with your child. Show examples of each.

☐ Work with your child to sort your dirty laundry into whites/colors.

☐ Let your child re-fold all the towels in your closet, stack them neatly, and put them back on the shelves.

☐ Have your child fold ten dish-towels or wash cloths all in the same way. Dish towels can be folded into thirds, wash cloths into quarters.

☐ Show your child how to operate your washing machine. If necessary, make a mark or put a sticker where the dial should go to begin the cycle.

☐ When training your child to vacuum, sprinkle baking soda, carpet freshener, or kitty litter over the floor and practice thoroughness.

☐ Make sure your child knows how to turn the vacuum on and off.

☐ Wash windows! Talk to your child about the materials you will need, gather them, and work systematically right to left.

☐ Practice stacking books and magazines: big on the bottom, small on the top.

☐ Let your child wipe off the table after a meal. Stress systematic left to right cleaning. Use a spray cleaner— this will help your child see where to wipe.

Parents,

Above is a suggested calendar of skills for our unit on Laundry/Housekeeping skills. Please try to do seven out of ten of these activities with your child to enrich our work at school. Initial the skills you are able to complete and return the list by _____: Students who return the calendar with seven of ten items initialed will receive _____.

Thank you for your support,

_____

Vocabulary Words - Laundry/Houskeeping Unit

fold
sweep
washing
blanket
stain
room number
dirty
supplies
windows
pillowcases
danger zones
machinery:
    washer
    dryer
    linen press
    lint machine

stack
trash
mirrors
laundry bag
linen cart
towel
washcloth
bath mat
sheets
break room

clean
laundry
gloves
sort
lobby
soiled
hand towel
vacuum
pillow
damaged

Evaluation/Documentation

The evaluation and documentation instruments are included to help the teacher track the skills each student has attempted. They can be helpful when assessing goal achievement and formulating IEP goals and objectives. There are two different forms. The teacher may choose to use one or the other or both, depending on the needs of the class.

Laundry/Housekeeping
IEP Goals and Objectives

The student will. . .

- ☐ Demonstrate systematic cleaning skills
    - ☐ identifying what needs to be cleaned
    - ☐ top-bottom, left-right
    - ☐ sweeping, vacuuming
    - ☐ identify and use cleaning materials
    - ☐ prepare materials and follow directions

- ☐ Demonstrate ability to fold and stack laundry appropriately
    - ☐ sorting: color, style, function, clean/dirty
    - ☐ folding: towels, washcloths, handtowels, bathmats, etc.
    - ☐ stacking a certain amount/number

- ☐ Demonstrate general cleaning skills:
    - ☐ surfaces: mirrors, windows, counters, tables
    - ☐ replace items in correct place after cleaning
    - ☐ parking lot and grounds cleanup
    - ☐ stock carts with supplies to take to other locations

- ☐ Demonstrate ability to systematically clean a room:
    - ☐ bedroom (strip and remake bed)
    - ☐ office
    - ☐ bathroom (sink, toilet, tub)

Evaluation/Documentation Laundry/Housekeeping Unit
Individual Student Format

Student's Name _____ Objectives	worksheet	worksheet	worksheet	practice	worksheet	activity	activity	community	overlay	overlay			
1. Demonstrate systematic cleaning skills													
identifying what needs to be cleaned													
top-bottom, left-right													
sweeping, vacuuming													
identify and use cleaning materials													
prepare materials and follow directions													
2. Ability to fold & stack laundry													
sorting: color, style, function, clean/dirty													
folding:													
towels, washcloths, hand towels, etc.													
stacking a certain amount/number													
3. Demonstrate general cleaning skills:													
surfaces: mirrors, windows, counters, tables													
replace items in correct place after cleaning													
parking lot and grounds cleanup													
stock carts with supplies													
4. Ability to systematically clean a room:													
bedroom (strip and remake bed)													
office													
bathroom (sink, toilet, tub)													

Evaluation/Documentation: Laundry/Housekeeping Unit
Total Class Format

Objectives	students																
1. Demonstrate systematic cleaning skills																	
Recognizing clean & dirty																	
Sorting clean & dirty clothes																	
Sweeping																	
Vacuuming																	
Recognizing cleaning vocabulary words																	
2. Demonstrate ability to sort, fold & stack laundry																	
Sorting clean & dirty items																	
Folding and stacking laundry items																	
Counting stacked items																	
Recognizing laundry vocabulary words																	
3. Demonstrate general cleaning skills																	
Demonstrate left-right, top-bottom cleaning																	
Cleaning mirrors																	
Cleaning windows																	
Cleaning table tops and counters																	
Replacing items after cleaning counters																	
Stocking cleaning carts																	
Using a checklist																	
Cleaning a parking lot																	
Recognizing cleaning vocabulary words																	
4. A. Skills needed to clean an office or public area																	
Emptying and relining trash cans																	
B. Skills needed to clean a bedroom																	
Stripping and remaking beds																	
C. Skills needed to clean a bathroom																	
Cleaning sinks and toilets																	
D. General information for cleaning a room																	
Correct cleaning order																	

Clean/Dirty Overlay

clean

dirty

Clean/Dirty and
Yes/No Overlay

clean

dirty

yes

no

Yes / No Overlay

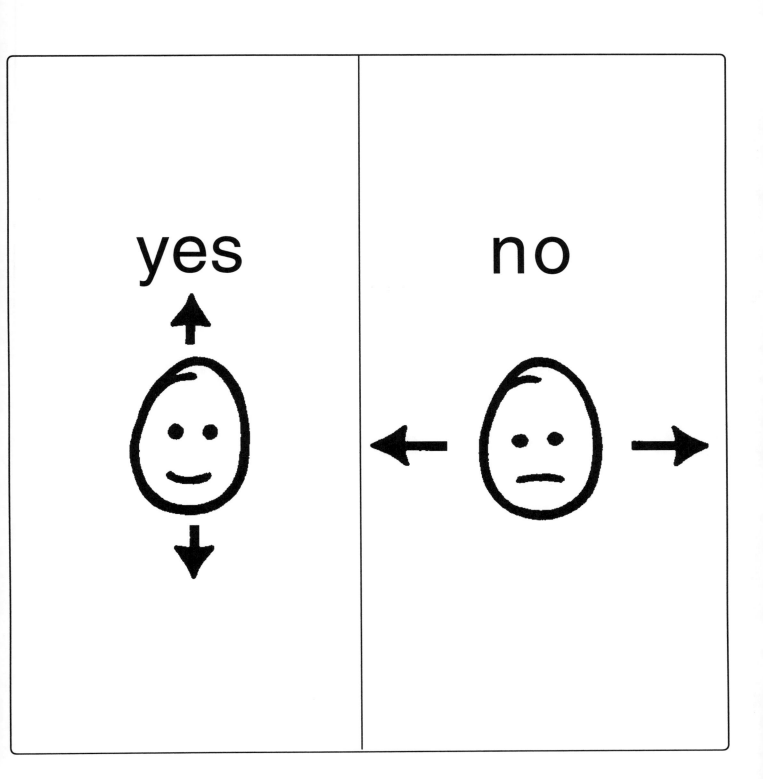

Laundry / Housekeeping Unit

Systematic Cleaning Skills

Laundry/Housekeeping: Objective 1

Student will demonstrate systematic cleaning skills.

Overview

Cleaning is an important part of almost any job, but it is especially important in the areas of laundry and housekeeping. These are two distinct job clusters but many of the skills are similar. These are the skills necessary to systematically clean in the following matter:

■ Top to bottom
■ Left to right
■ Following a certain order

The concept of systematic cleaning is a difficult one for many students with disabilities. The lessons included in this objective will address training and assistive techniques to help students complete systematic cleaning.

Suggested Activities

Is It Clean Or Dirty?

The first step in cleaning is to be able to discriminate between **clean** and **dirty**. Practice and experience are the only way to teach/learn this skill.

Skill: *Recognizing which items are clean and which are dirty.*
Activity: Start with white items, such as T-shirts, hankies, washcloths, or just white pieces of fabric. Make some of the items obviously dirty—very dirty so that there is no question that they are dirty. Begin teaching the concept of **clean** and **dirty**. Use the **Clean & Dirty Activity Page**, 198, and the **Clean/Dirty and Yes/No Overlay**, page 190, with this concept. There will be more opportunity to practice this in the next objective (Ability to sort, fold, and stack laundry).

Worksheet — Clean or Dirty?
The **Clean Or Dirty worksheet,** page 199, is designed to provide additional practice in sorting clean and dirty clothes. Students are asked to make an "X" on the dirty items. For students who are unable to use a pencil or marker, stamps can be adapted for use. Students who are unable to physically use stamps can be paired with another student and answer yes/no questions using the **Clean/Dirty and Yes/No Overlay,** page 190.

Picture Perfect

Skill: *More recognizing which items are clean and which are dirty.*
Activity: Have each student bring in a piece of clothing that can be dirtied without getting in trouble. Take a picture of each piece of clothing while it is clean. Then conduct an activity that is certain to get the clothing dirty; e.g., painting, washing a car, moving trash, etc. Have the film developed with double prints. (Take a few pictures of the students wearing the clothing clean and dirty just for fun.) Make a copy of the **Clean/Dirty Activity Page,** page 198, laminate it, and cut it apart. Tape each piece on a small container (a box, paper bag, plastic organizer tray, etc.) Then have the students sort the photos into the clean or dirty basket.

Worksheet — Sorting Clean Clothes
The **Sorting Clothes Worksheet,** page 200, makes a good homework follow-up to the previous activities. It offers students a chance to show parents what they have been learning at school and to practice those concepts at the same time. Be sure to send home to parents any special adaptations that the student used at school.

Faster And Faster

Skill: *Sorting clean and dirty clothes with increasing speed.*
Activity: Repeat the first activity, **Is It Clean Or Dirty?** many times. Remember that students need to learn to work continuously for 45 minutes or longer before taking a break. If the student masters the clean/dirty concept, then focus on increasing speed while maintaining accuracy. The **Data Collection Worksheet,** page 201, may be helpful for record keeping. The top portion is designed for students to complete and the bottom is for teachers. Fold the page in half or cut it apart if it is too distracting for the student.

Sweeping

This is a very difficult skill for many students and yet it is a skill that is helpful and even necessary for success in many vocational settings. Often the dirty area to be cleaned is not easy to determine. Imaginary or invisible dirt is very hard for many students to clean and yet, it is essential that they develop a practice of sweeping systematically whether they can see the dirt or not.

Skill: *Sweeping the floor.*
Activity: Use cat litter or baking soda sprinkled on the ground. Teach the left to right concept.

Push Or Pull

Skill: *Identifying the correct broom to use.*
Activity: This activity is designed to introduce students to the two main types of brooms and their general uses. Keep at least one of each type of broom in the classroom for discussion and for practice. In this initial activity, demonstrate correct use of each broom by pouring course sand (beans, cat litter, etc.) on the floor and correctly sweeping up the mess.

Worksheet — Which Broom Do You Use?

Use the **Which Broom Do You Use? Worksheet**, page 202, to discuss where to use each type of broom or use this worksheet as a take home activity.

A Picture Is Worth 1000 Words

Skill: *Taking picture of areas that need to be swept.*
Activity: On the next community-based instruction trip, let students take photos of areas that would need to be swept by an employee (be sure to clear this ahead of time with the store manager—sometimes they are very touchy about photos). If possible, get photos of employees sweeping to use for classroom display. Let students take some photos, but be sure you or some other adults takes a set of back-up photos in case the students don't quite focus or center pictures. Use these photos to make a bulletin-board display or poster showing where and how different types of brooms are used. (If you do not have access to community-based instruction, you will have to take the photos at another time or ask a store manager to do it for you.)

Vacuuming

Skill: *Using a vacuum to clean the floor.*
Activity: Read the discussion under the first **Sweeping** activity, page 195. The basic concepts are the same, only the tools are different. Have a vacuum cleaner available in the classroom for demonstration and practice. For students who have difficulty vacuuming a large space, use masking tape to divide the floor into squares or areas of more manageable size. You may want to sprinkle carpet freshener or cat litter so that students can see where to vacuum.

Poster

Make a poster using pictures of vacuum cleaners from magazines, newspapers, and junk mail. This is an excellent homework assignment: bring in one or more pictures of a vacuum cleaner. Contact a local vacuum cleaner sales office and see if they have brochures they will donate. Don't overlook warehouse merchandisers or large discount stores.

How Do I Turn It Off?

Skill: *Using on/off switch on the vacuum cleaner.*
Activity: Demonstrate on the vacuum cleaner in your classroom. Stress the use of the on/off switch instead of pulling the plug. Show as many different vacuum cleaners as possible to help students generalize.

Worksheet — On/Off Practice
The **On/Off Worksheet**, page 203, is designed to practice the left-to-right concept and reinforce the words "on" and "off." Have students put their pencils on the box with a number in it and move to the right, stopping at the first "off" and marking it with an "X." If necessary, color the number box with a green marker as a cue.

Worksheet — Safety First
The **Safety First Worksheet,** page 204, reinforces safety procedures. It also makes a good take- home activity page. Students answer safety questions with a yes/no response. The yes/no response is difficult for many students. It is a very important skill to practice.

Advanced Vacuum Cleaning

Students need to learn to vacuum as they walk backwards or "out of a room" so they do not leave footprints on the carpet. Hotels are very strict about this.

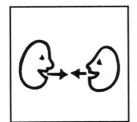

Vocabulary, Vocabulary, Vocabulary

The following words are used when sweeping and vacuum floors.

clean	dirty	off
sweep	sort	on
vacuum	safety	speed

Use the **Vocabulary Practice Worksheet,** page 205, for this activity. Go over each word with the students. Use concrete objects and demonstrations to be sure the students can use the words or understand their use. After discussion, students can practice writing by copying the words.

Clean/Dirty Activity Page

Teacher Directions: Make a copy of this page then laminate and cut apart. Tape each on a small containter or box and have students sort clean and dirty items into the correct container.

Worksheet
Clean Or Dirty?

Name _____ Date _____

Directions: Put an "X" on the dirty items.

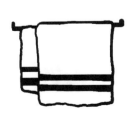  

Laundry / Housekeeping Unit

Worksheet
Sorting Clothes

Name _____ Date _____

Directions: Sort the clothes. Draw a line from each piece of clothing to the clean basket, if the clothes are clean, or to the dirty basket, if the clothes are dirty.

Worksheet
Data Collection

Student fills out the top half.

Name _____ Date _____

how many		Start Time	Stop Time

washcloth			
towel			

Teacher fills out the lower half.

Name _____ Date _____

Start Time	Stop Time	Total Minutes	# Items	# Per Min.	# Correct

Laundry / Housekeeping Unit

Worksheet
Which Broom Do You Use?

Name _____ Date _____

broom

push broom

small areas

parking lot

store

loading dock

wide hallways

inside aisles

under tables

Worksheet
On/Off Left to Right

Name _____ Date _____

Put your pencil on a square with a number in it. Go across the line from left to right. Put an "X" on the **very first** "OFF" you see.

| Left | ➡️ | Right |

| 1 | ON OFF OFF ON ON OFF |

| 2 | ON ON ON ON OFF ON ON |

| 3 | OFF OFF OFF OFF OFF |

| 4 | ON ON ON ON ON OFF ON |

| 5 | ON ON ON ON ON OFF ON |

| 6 | ON OF FFO FO OFF OFF OF |

Laundry / Housekeeping Unit

Worksheet
Safety Practice

Name ————————————— Date ———————

Directions: Read the sentences below and circle the correct answer.

———————————————————————————————————————

1. You should be very careful with electric plugs.

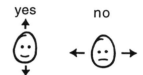

2. It is OK to put your fingers in an electrical plug.

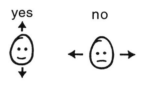

3. It is OK to turn your vacuum cleaner off by pulling out the plug.

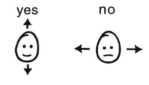

4. You should hold the plug by the rubber part.

5. You should always be careful with electricity.

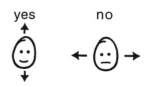

6. The safest way to turn off a vacuum cleaner is with the on/off switch.

Worksheet
Vocabulary Practice

Name _____ Date _____

The following words are important if you have a job in the Laundry/Housekeeping area. Talk about each word and then write it for practice.

clean	dirty	off
_____	_____	_____

sweep	sort	on
_____	_____	_____

vacuum	safety	speed
_____	_____	_____

Sort, Fold, Stack

Laundry/Housekeeping: Objective 2

Student will demonstrate the ability to sort, fold, and stack laundry appropriately.

Overview

This is a task that many people find boring. However, in a hospital or hotel, laundry workers will sort and fold for two or more hours straight without taking a break. This task should also be done standing up to develop stamina and endurance. Very few jobs allow workers to sit and work. Tasks should be set up so the students work a minimum of 45 minutes.

Suggested Activities

Clean Or Dirty?

Skill: *Sorting clean and dirty items.*
Activity: Sort washcloths into clean and dirty stacks. Begin with washrags or dishcloths that are obviously dirty or torn. Mix them with clean ones so identification is easy. You will need to have as many as possible for this activity. Use the **Clean/Dirty or Clean/Dirty and Yes/No Overlay,** pages 189-190.

This task can be done quickly by most students, however there are people who perform this task all day in commercial type laundries, hospitals, and motels.

Worksheet — More Clean/Dirty Practice
The **More Clean/Dirty Practice Worksheet,** page 211, offers additional practice in the concept of sorting clean and dirty laundry and makes an excellent home assignment to involve parents in the skills being learned at school. It is only intended to be an additional activity, not a replacement for hands-on activities that train and allow for practice. Students are asked to sort clean and dirty laundry by drawing a line from each bin.

Worksheet — Where's the Spot?

This worksheet, page 212, offers a chance to combine the skill of discerning clean and dirty with some fine motor activity. Students who cannot use a pencil or marker can be given an adapted stamp for marking or can be paired with another student and use the **Clean/Dirty and Yes/ No Overlay**, page 190, to communicate the correct marking. Students are to make a mark on the dirty area of each piece of laundry.

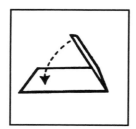

Fold The Laundry

Skill: *Stacking washcloths.*
Activity: Washcloths can be stacked flat (hospital use) or folded in half (hotel use). Teach the stacking method first. After that is mastered, move on to folding in half.

Worksheet — Sorting Laundry

The **Sorting Laundry Worksheet,** page 213, provides another chance to practice sorting towels and other laundry items. Again, this makes an excellent take-home assignment for parental involvement and student communication. Be sure to send home any adaptions and/or overlays used in class. Students are to draw a line from each piece of laundry to the correct table to stack it on.

Discussion Picture - Folding Laundry

Use the line drawing of two employees folding towels, page 214, as a discussion starter for the task of folding laundry. This is a good chance to review vocabulary and identification of laundry items.

Folding Laundry
Discussion Picture

Sorting Laundry

One of the basic laundry tasks is sorting clean laundry. You will need several of each item—towels, washcloths, sheets, etc., in a basket for students to sort.

Skill: *Sorting laundry.*
Activity: Have ten or more of each item for ample practice (washcloths, towels, T-shirts, etc.). If sorting is difficult, use colored objects for initial training; i.e., have all towels blue, all washcloths white, etc. Then make discriminations more difficult as task is mastered.

Laundry Blues

Teach students to fold their own clothes in functional situations.

The Next Step Is Towels, Or You Want Me To Do What?

Towels are more difficult to fold. They are usually folded in thirds and then in half. Use the **Folding Towels Discussion Picture,** page 215, to help explain.

> **Skill**: *Folding towels.*
>
> **Activity:** Demonstrate, assist the student (hand over hand if necessary), and then model and practice. This is a very difficult task to learn. Allow the student to practice often, remembering that the person who performs this job must often fold towels for two hours before taking a break. You will need at least 24 items (2 dozen) , more if possible, to simulate this work task. If this task is difficult, begin with towels or washcloths. Team uniforms are a good item to practice on. Some teachers have students do the uniform laundry and then fold and deliver. Food service labs and the cafeteria are also good sources for laundry to fold.

How Many in a Stack?

Once folding is mastered, have students stack a certain amount of items (e.g., five washcloths, ten towels, etc.). Students who cannot count can be given a "jig" or paper where they mark an "X" for each item folded until the correct amount is reached.

Worksheet — Counting Stacks

The **Counting Stacks Worksheet,** page 216, is designed to allow additional practice in counting and writing the amount. If students do not know or cannot write their numbers, they can make marks or stack blocks for each towel they "count." This is a good opportunity to teach students an effective way to end up with the correct amount even if they cannot count.

Teamwork

This is a good activity to pair a variety of levels together. One student can sort items into stacks (towels, washcloths, hand towels, etc.), one student can fold washcloths, one student can fold towels, one student can count out items and stack them, and one student can take them and put the stacks on shelves or carts.

Role Play
Use the **Role Play Activity**, page 217, to discuss the importance of doing a job correctly. This skill could have significant impact on future employment. After the role play is completed, there are follow-up questions, page 218, for individual or group work. There is a **Role Play Overlay**, page 219 to assist with this activity.

Worksheet — Counting Towels
The **Counting Towels Worksheet,** page 220, worksheet is designed to give extra practice to counting stacked laundry. Be creative in adapting the worksheet to suit the skills and needs of individual students. This worksheet is meant to be an idea starter for worksheets that can be made on Boardmaker for individual students. The students are asked to count the towels and draw a line from the towels to the correct number. The numbers could be cut out and glued onto blocks to make it easier for students to pick them up and move them to the correct stack. Remember that a student who cannot physically fold towels may be able to work in an enclave to assist other students count or keep track of work done.

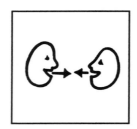

Vocabulary, Vocabulary, Vocabulary
Use the **Vocabulary Words Worksheet,** page 221, to provide practice with writing vocabulary words that relate to laundry skills. The words are:

clean	dirty	count
towels	sort	stack
laundry		

For students who learn well visually, you may want to consider drawing boxes in the shapes of the letters (tall, short, below the line, etc.)
Example:

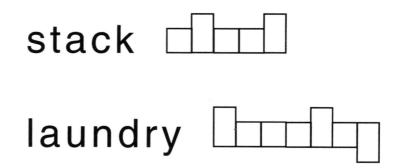

Worksheet
More Clean/Dirty Practice

Name _____ Date _____

Directions: Draw a line from the mats to the correct laundry bin: Clean or Dirty.

Laundry / Housekeeping Unit

Worksheet
Where's The Spot?

Name _____ Date _____

Directions: Circle the dirty spot on each mat.

Worksheet
Sorting Laundry

Name _____ Date _____

Directions: Sort the clean laundry to the correct table to be folded.

Laundry / Housekeeping Unit

Folding Laundry Discussion Picture

Folding Towels Discussion Picture

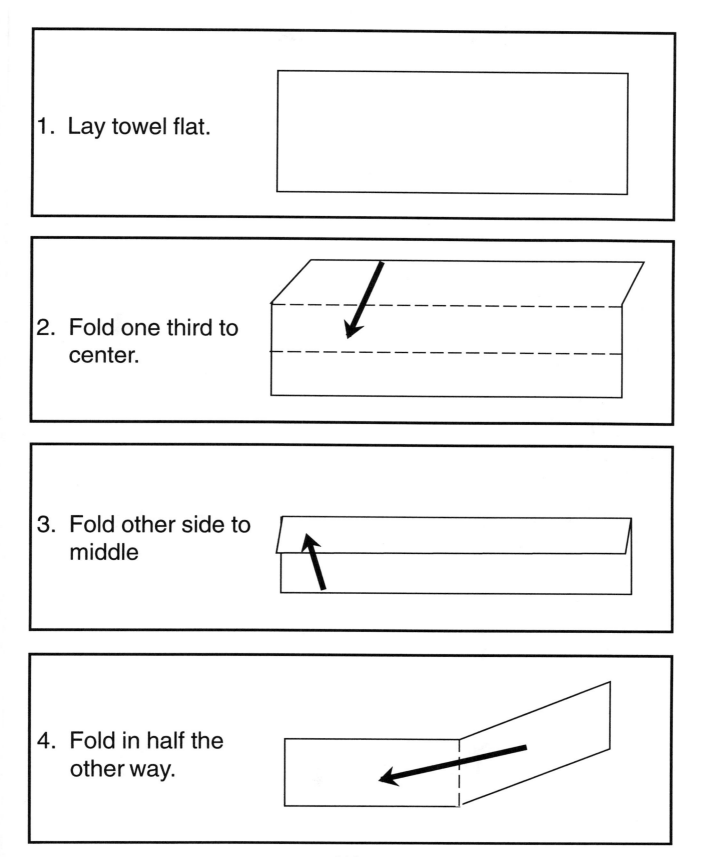

1. Lay towel flat.

2. Fold one third to center.

3. Fold other side to middle

4. Fold in half the other way.

Worksheet
Counting Stacks

Name _____ Date _____

Directions: Count the towels stacked on the tables and write the number in the box on the right.

Role Play - Laundry/Housekeeping

(Use with Role Play Overlay, page 219)

The following conversation takes place in a commercial laundry:

Bill: Sue, here are some more towels for your stack—hey, why are you folding yours THAT way? Mrs. James told us to fold them into thirds.

Sue: Well, I don't care what that old bat says. Her glasses are so thick that she wouldn't be able to see my towels if they were as big as a barn. Besides, I'm mad at her. She wouldn't let me have the day off tomorrow. My boyfriend is coming into town next week and I need to get my nails done. I can't believe she is being so unfair. So, I'll just fold my little towels any way I please.

Bill: But Sue, don't you think you should do it the right way? It's not really any harder and it won't help you to have Mrs. James mad at you.

Sue: I don't care if she is mad at me—she can just get over it. These towels are stupid anyway. I hate folding them. I am tired of this old job. I hope she gets mad and fires me.

Bill: That's not such a great idea, Sue. I thought you needed this job.

Sue: Well, I need a job, but maybe not this one.

Bill: But Sue, if you get fired, you will have a really hard time getting another one.

Sue: What are you talking about?

Bill: When you apply for a job, they ask you where you have worked before, right?

Sue: Yeah, so what?

Bill: So they call up your last boss and ask what kind of worker you were. If a place you want to work finds out you were fired for not doing your job right, the new place might not want to hire you.

Sue: *(Beginning to refold her towels)* Wow! I never thought about it that way. If I want a different job, I had better do this one well so that I will get a good reference.

(Some hours later)

Mrs. James: It's almost time to go, Sue. Let me have the last of your towels. These look very nice. You have made some good improvements. If you keep this up, you may be in for a raise soon.

Sue: A raise? What are you talking about?

Mrs. James: Haven't you been with us almost six months? Employees are evaluated after their first six months with us. If your work has been satisfactory, you are offered a raise.

Sue: I didn't know that! Wow!

Mrs. James: I hope you have a good visit with your boyfriend, Sue. Good-bye now!

Sue: Bye, Mrs. James.

Role Play Questions

1. Why did Bill tell Sue to fold her towels a different way?
   a. Bill knows how the boss wants them done.
   b. Bill is just too picky and wants everything his way.
   c. Bill does not like Sue and always gives her a hard time.

2. Sue is thinking about getting another job. What kind of advice does Bill give Sue about getting another job?
   a. She should just quit.
   b. She should do good work at this job so that she will get a good recommendation for her next job.
   c. She should tell the next job's boss why she didn't like her first job.

3. What did Sue find out about people who do good work at the laundry?
   a. They have to work a long time.
   b. They get a party.
   c. They get a raise.

4. Who is Mrs. James?
   a. She is Sue's mom.
   b. She is Sue's best friend.
   c. She is Sue's boss.

5. Do you think Sue will keep her job? Why?

Role Play Overlay

a	b	c
yes	I don't know	no
fold	money	paycheck

Worksheet
Counting Towels

Name _____ Date _____

Directions: Count the towels in the box on the left and draw a line to the correct number on the right.

_____

(3 towels)	**3**
(5 towels)	**5**
(2 towels)	**2**
(4 towels)	**4**
(1 towel)	**6**

Worksheet
Vocabulary Words

Name _____   Date _____

Directions: Write the words.

clean	clean	
dirty	dirty	
count	count	
towel	towels	
sort	sort	
	stack	
laundry	laundry	

Laundry / Housekeeping Unit

General Cleaning Skills

Overview

General cleaning skills are used in almost all job settings. This is also one of the most difficult skills to teach intellectually disabled students. Practice in a variety of settings with a variety of trainers is the most effective method of teaching these skills. These activities are designed to give some ideas of ways to practice while in the classroom or school setting. Encourage parents to support these skills at home. The concept of cleaning "top-to-bottom, left-to-right" is critical to cleaning. It cannot be over emphasized, stated, or practiced. It needs to become an automatic response to the directions to clean.

Suggested Activities

Remember And Review
Review the clean and dirty concepts from the previous objectives. Emphasize the need for cleaning correctly. Discuss types of jobs where cleaning is necessary.

Mirror, Mirror
Demonstrate left-to-right, top-to-bottom cleaning on a hanging mirror (a bathroom mirror is usually stable; if you do not have a mirror hanging in your room, seriously consider having a mirror securely mounted in your room to help students learn self-monitoring). Introduce either the **Top-Bottom/Right-Left Overlay 1 or 2,** pages 229-230, and use with all window and mirror cleaning activities.

The Cleaning Game
Skill: *Cleaning windows and mirrors using the top-bottom, right-left technique.*
Activity: Divide group into two teams. Have Team 1 put their heads down (or leave the room) and let Team 2 smudge the mirror. Team-1 then selects someone to correctly clean the mirror (*top to bottom,*

The Cleaning Game (continued)

left to right). Team 2 determines if it was correctly cleaned. Then switch sides. Start out with obvious smudges, i.e., lipstick, food, etc., and talk students through the process. Then progress to less obvious smudges (dirty fingers, hand cream, etc.) without prompting.

HINT: Make a checklist of correct procedure and let the teams score each other on specific items.

Windows and Mirrors

Most window cleaners spray on clear even if they appear colored in the container. Put one or two drops of food coloring into the window cleaner to make it easier to see while training (don't put more than a drop or two because it can stain wood and fabric). This is a good time to see if students can actually operate a spray container which is a very difficult motor skill and may need to be practiced. Use the **Window Washing Discussion Picture,** page 231, for this activity.

Window Washing Discussion Picture

Worksheet — Find the Dirt

This worksheet on page 232, is designed to give students practice in finding dirty areas on a mirror or window. There is no substitute for hands-on cleaning activities, but this will provide a classroom or homework activity to help generalize skills. Students are asked to locate and circle the dirty area on mirrors and windows.

Hand-Over-Hand

Skill: *Using the left-right, top-bottom method to clean windows.*
Activity: Do initial instruction hand-over-hand, then model. Repeat the phrase "left to right, top to bottom" often so it becomes an automatic part of the cleaning process. Don't accept sloppy work. Give feedback like "that was a good try, let me help you clean it the right way." Accepting sloppy work during training will transfer to sloppy work on the job. Use the **Top-Bottom, Left-Right, Overlays,** pages 229-230, with this activity.

Worksheet — Left To Right

The **Left To Right Worksheet,** page 233, is designed to offer practice with the "left-to-right, top-to-bottom: skill. Using a wide marker, (a transparent highlighter would be perfect), start in the top LEFT corner on the "X". Go left to right, pick up the marker and go to the next row and go left-to-right again. Continue until "mirrored" surface is covered with marker "marks."

Table Tops And Counters

Skill: More Left To Right, Top Top Bottom practice.
Activity: Spread shaving cream or whipped cream on other surfaces to train. Continue to emphasize "left to right, top to bottom." *Hint:* Use the shaving cream sparingly—it makes a real mess. Use sticky substances that are easy to check for cleanliness: jelly, syrup, honey, etc. Students should learn to clean the entire table or surface even if it doesn't **look** dirty. Also encourage speed—this needs to be a quick and thorough wipe, not an hour long process on one table.

Worksheet — What To Clean?

Use the **What To Clean Worksheet,** page 234, as a discussion starter in addition to a group activity. Students are asked to determine which things they might have to clean at work. Accept any answer if the student can give an example. Students can pantomime cleaning the item and have other students guess which one they are cleaning.

School Cafeteria Duty

Have the students clean tables and chairs after lunch. This is a real task and provides practice in systematic cleaning with a purpose. Check with your custodial staff—most are happy to have help with any cleaning activity. Remember, this is a teaching activity. Students should be closely monitored so that training can be provided as needed.(This is not time to get a cup of coffee.) It is also important to collect data on this training process. This type of data provides feedback for the students, documentation for the teacher, and information on training and progress for the parents. This data is also helpful to adult service providers when they are making job placement decisions. Students who have mastered this skill to an independent level can help supervise the other students and complete the data sheets. Use the **Sample Data Sheet,** page 235, for this purpose. Adapt this data sheet to individual student needs.

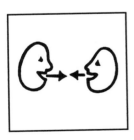

Vocabulary, Vocabulary, Vocabulary

Use the **Vocabulary Practice Worksheet,** page 236, to review vocabulary and symbols as well as reading and writing skills. Don't forget to look for ways to allow all students to participate. (Cut apart sections and glue onto blocks for matching.)

spray	dirty	top
bottom	left	right
wipe	window	mirror
clean		

Worksheet - More Vocabulary Practice
The **Vocabulary Practice Worksheet,** page 237, focuses on vocabulary for this unit. Students are asked to write the words. This list provides an opportunity to discuss the meaning of words. It also makes a good homework page to inform parents of the student's progress.

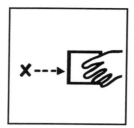

Where Does It Go?

In most cleaning tasks, items on a table top or counter must be moved to clean the surface and then returned to their correct positions. One way to do this is to photograph the items in their correct position and use the photo to replace items. (See **Grocery Store Unit,** Stacking Activities With Photos, page 26). If photo system is mastered, progress to line drawings or symbols, and then to words if possible. Checklists can have line drawings added to help students do work correctly.

Picture This

Skill: *Replacing items on table or counter top.*
Activity: Set up five or more areas with up to ten items. You can use fewer items for those who need it—even one-to-one matching (see next task). Use items that might be found in a bathroom that would be cleaned on a job: shampoo bottle, soap, cup(s), matchbook (don't forget to remove the matches), ashtray, tissue box, small ice bucket, water pitcher, toothbrush, tube of toothpaste, small tray, small "tent" sign, pencil, etc. Arrange these items and take a photo of them in the desired position. Then put them into a lidded box with the photo. Label the box with a "stock number" so the students can locate their assignment. Give them a card with the assignment number on it or give them verbal directions if they can follow them. They then take the box and the photo and set up the area correctly. Prepare as many boxes as possible with a variety of items to allow practice. Large shoe boxes work very well. Contact your local discount stores and ask them to save you boot boxes.

Worksheet—Match The Counter
This worksheet, page 238, is designed to provide practice in using a diagram to return items to a counter correctly. Students are asked to look at the sample counter and mark the counters that are correct. This makes a good take-home assignment for generalization activities with parents.

Stocking Carts or How do I get all this stuff there?

Most jobs that involve cleaning on a routine basis have a cart or other container to carry the cleaning materials from one place to another in an efficient manner. The most common is a cleaning cart. In hotels there is a list of materials that should be on the cart, although most workers just stock from looking at a completed cart. The following activities are designed to help students learn to set up a cleaning cart independently.

Make This One Look Like That One

Skill: *Stocking a cleaning cart.*
Activity: Set up a rolling cart (a media cart works well) with cleaning items that might be needed in cleaning a room (see **Suggested Cleaning Items** for ideas, page 239). Give the student a box of materials that includes those items on the other cart plus some extra items not needed. Ask the student to set up a second cart to look like the first one. If this task is too difficult for the students, you can put photos or line drawings of each item on the second cart and let the student do one-to-one matching. The goal of this activity is independence, so experiment with the cue that the student needs to do this task independently.

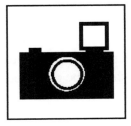

More Picture Perfect

Skill: *Stocking a cleaning cart from a photo.*
Activity: Take a photo of a cart that has been correctly set up and ask the student to set up a second cart like the photo. Start out with just the correct items and mix in extra items as the task is mastered.

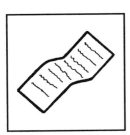

Checking The List Twice

Many jobs that involve routine cleaning have a checklist for employees to follow. In jobs where employees often use English as a second language, employers have begun to add line drawings to the list so that it is clear what is needed. This system works very well for students who cannot read well enough to follow a written list. See page 253, for sample of a picture checklist.

Skill: *Stocking a cleaning cart from a picture checklist.*
Activity: Give students a box of cleaning materials and a picture checklist of what should be on the cleaning cart and have them set up the cart.

Don't Forget The Experts

The maintenance staff in your school are readily available experts. They have been trained in a variety of safety and cleaning techniques. Ask them to demonstrate or let students observe them working. Most people like to be the expert and welcome an opportunity to teach others. Ask them to show their cleaning supplies and explain how they know which one to use when.

Parking Lot And Grounds Cleanup

Many jobs involve taking a turn at cleaning the parking lot or other outside areas. This is a skill that can be easily practiced on most school campuses. Parking lot safety is essential!

Skill: *Cleaning the parking lot.*

Activity: One of the most difficult parts of this task is using the dustpan with a long handle to sweep up cigarette butts and small pieces of trash. Ask your maintenance staff if you can borrow their dustpan for practice. This skill can be practiced inside, but it will need to be practiced outside as well. It is also critical that students learn that this job must still be done in the cold and in the rain, not just when it's nice. It's also not a time to be silly and play. Review parking lot safety often.

Worksheet — Parking Lot Clean Up

Students are asked to look at the outdoor scene, page 240, and mark the trash that needs to be picked up. This worksheet makes a good discussion picture or homework assignment. When talking about what needs to be picked up, also discuss where the trash should be disposed of. Use adapted stamps to mark selections for students that need physical assistance. The **Top-Bottom, Right-Left Overlay,** page 229, can be used with this worksheet.

Worksheet — Clean-Up Questions

Using the Clean-Up Questions Worksheet, page 241, students are asked to answer questions with a yes/no response. Answering yes/no questions can be difficult for intellectually disabled students, yet it is the type of question most often asked in the work setting. This is a critical skill on any job.

Worksheet — More Vocabulary Review

In the **More Vocabulary Review Worksheet,** page 242, students are asked to pick the word that best completes a sentence. Don't forget to make adaptations for students who can't do this as a paper/pencil activity.

Top-Bottom / Right-Left Overlay 1

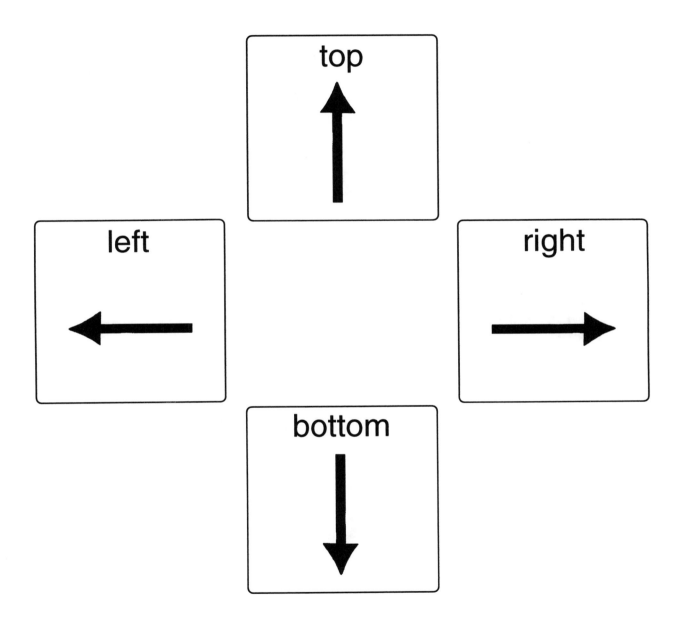

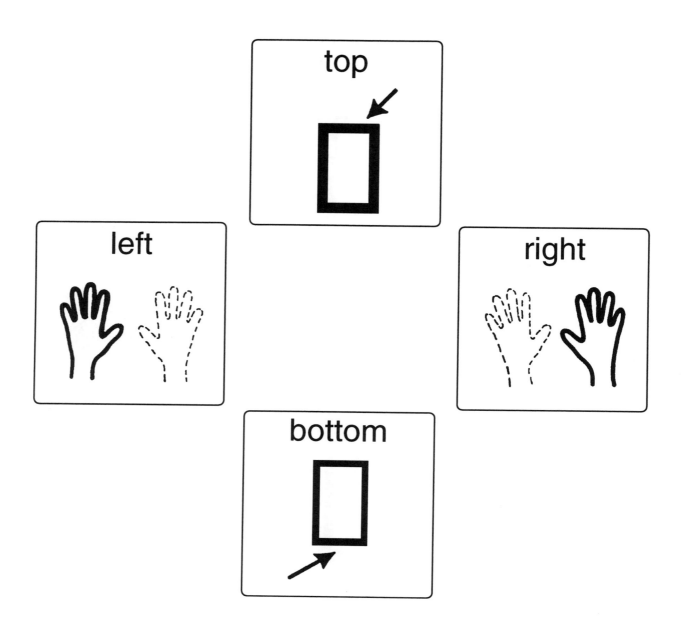

Window Cleaning Discussion Picture

Laundry / Housekeeping Unit

Worksheet
Find The Dirt

Name _____ Date _____

Directions: Look carefully at these mirrors and windows. Circle any dirty spots you see.

 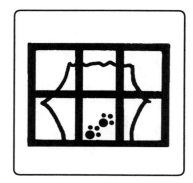 

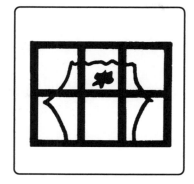  

Worksheet
Left To Right

Name _____ Date _____

Directions: Using a marker, start at the top left corner on the "X." Draw a mark from left to right. Pick up the marker and go to the next row and repeat until mirror is covered with marks.

X

X

X

X

X

X

X

X

X

X

X

X

Laundry / Housekeeping Unit

Worksheet
What To Clean?

Name _____ Date _____

Directions: Look at the words below. Mark the things that you might clean at work.

shoes	car	mirror
dog	chair	
window	sink	teeth
microwave	table	

Sample Data Sheet

Name _____ Date _____

	Needs No Help	With Reminders	With Help	Not Done
Clean 5 tables				
Set 8 chairs at each table				
Throw away trash				
Work without talking				

Name _____ Date _____

table
good   bad

table
good   bad

table
good   bad

table
good   bad

table
good   bad

table
good   bad

Worksheet
Vocabulary Practice

Name _____ Date _____

Directions: Match the words to the correct symbol, then write the word.

Symbol	Word	
clean	**mirror**	
dirty	**left**	
mirror	**top**	
window	**clean**	
left	**window**	
right	**dirty**	
top	**bottom**	
bottom	**right**	

Worksheet
More Vocabulary Practice

Name_____ Date_____

Directions: Write the word.

spray	**spray**	
dirty	**dirty**	
top	**top**	
bottom	**bottom**	
left	**left**	
right	**right**	
wipe	**wipe**	

Worksheet
Match the Counter

Name_____ Date_____

Directions: Look at the counter top in the box. Circle any other counters that look exactly like the first counter.

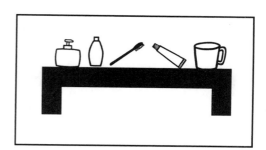

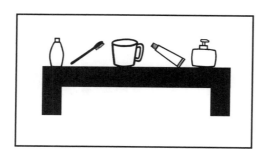

Suggested Cleaning Items
For Stocking A Cart

✔ Containers that are clearly marked.

✔ Powdered cleaners such as Comet®, Windex®, etc.

✔ Bathroom cleaners that are not aerosol cans.

✔ Toilet brush.

✔ Carpet freshener or baking soda.

✔ Spray for dusting — furniture polish.

✔ A variety of cleaners to help match and make choices.

Hint: Make photos of each product to have on hand for photo books if needed later.

Worksheet
Parking Lot Cleanup

Name_____ Date_____

Directions: Look at the picture below. Put an "X" on any trash that needs to be picked up. Draw a circle around the right places to put the trash.

Worksheet
Cleanup Questions

Name_____ Date_____

Directions: Read the sentences and pick [yes ☺] or [no ☹] .

1. If the boss is not looking, it is OK not to clean carefully.　　[yes] [no]

2. If a table doesn't look dirty, it is OK not to wipe it.　　[yes] [no]

3. It is OK to wipe all the dirt from the table to the floor without sweeping it up.　　[yes] [no]

4. If the boss asks you to clear off a table, it is OK to wait a while.　　[yes] [no]

5. To make sure you clean the whole table, first wipe the sides and then the middle.　　[yes] [no]

6. If you are mopping the floor and it is time for your break, finish the floor first.　　[yes] [no]

Worksheet
Vocabulary Review

Name_____ Date_____

Directions: Put the words or pictures in the correct place to complete the sentences.

dirty	cleaning	bottom	wipe	right

1. [ ] is important in many jobs.

2. If something is not clean, it is [ ].

3. It is important to clean from left to [ ]

   and from top to [ ].

4. [ ] carefully to get the whole surface clean.

General Cleaning Skills

Overview Objectives 4A - 4D

Some jobs require more specific cleaning skills. The following activities are designed to provide training and practice in many general cleaning skills. They have been grouped into three basic groups:

- Skills needed to clean an office or other public area
- Skills needed to clean a bedroom
- Skills needed to clean a bathroom

There is no substitute for hands-on cleaning in real settings. These skills and activities are not meant to be exhaustive or even representative. They were selected with the primary consideration of classroom participation. These activities should be expanded as much as possible in your particular setting.

These skills are more difficult to adapt for the physically impaired. This does not mean these students should be left out of these activities. It does mean you will have to be creative. Enlist your students in developing adaptions. They are often more creative and it is good practice in problem solving.

The general cleaning skills objectives are as follows:

Objective 4A — *Skills needed to clean an office or other public area.*

Objective 4B — *Skills needed to clean a bedroom.*

Objective 4C — *Skills needed to clean a bathroom.*

Objective 4D — *General information for cleaning a room.*

Office Cleaning Skills

Skills needed to clean an office or other public area.

Suggested Activities

Save Those Plastic Grocery Bags

Enlist students, parents, and other teachers in collecting plastic grocery bags to use as practice trash can liners (trash can liners are expensive and you will need a lot of them to master the skill). These are cheaper and the built-in handles on the plastic bags make it easier to learn to tie the bags closed.

Flip That Chart

Skill: *Recognizing trash can emptying sequence.*
Activity: Copy the **Flip Chart Pictures 1 & 2,** pages 249 & 250. Glue the pages onto construction paper or old file folders. Cut out each of the rectangles and laminate. Punch holes in the top and use two or three small metal rings to bind into a flip chart. (Check with your media center, teacher resource center, or art classes to see if they have a binding machine you can use.) Another option is to use a small photo album and put one section on each page. These pictures give the sequence of emptying trash cans. Still another option is to mount a strip of Velcro on wood or cardboard. Copy and laminate **Flip Chart Pictures 1 & 2,** cut out, and mount corresponding Velcro on the back. The pictures can be easily sequenced over and over. Self-adhesive Velcro strips can be purchased at some fabric stores.

What Do I Do First?

Skill: *More trash can emptying sequence practice.*
Activity: Copy the **Flip Chart Pictures 1 & 2,** pages 249 & 250. Mount on heavy paper or old file folders and cut out. Students can put these steps in order. This is excellent practice in sequencing and direction-following vocabulary: What do you do **first**? What do you do **next**?

Tie It!

Trash bags are usually tied closed in housekeeping settings to prevent spillage as carts are pushed around.

Skill: *Tying trash bags using a simple double knot.*
Activity: The most efficient way to tie a plastic bag is with a simple double knot. Recycled plastic grocery bags are the easiest to use. Once this is mastered, change to regular liners (a much more difficult task). If students are unable to tie the bags, they must have an effective way to ask for help!

Recycle Project

Most schools recycle aluminum drink cans. Talk to the person in charge and offer to collect the cans from lounges or other areas. Use small cans lined with trash bags to give students ample opportunity to practice tying up bags. If your school doesn't already recycle cans, look into it for a class project. It can be a moneymaking opportunity.

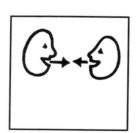

Vocabulary, Vocabulary, Vocabulary

The following are vocabulary words useful for the public area cleaning objective. Review the words with your students.

empty	trash	bag	clean
tie	careful	work	housekeeping
lift	full		

Worksheet — Vocabulary Practice Words

Using the worksheet on page 251, discuss each of the words, then students can practice writing the word if able. Students that cannot write could match words and symbols cut out from another sheet. Laminate two worksheets—cut out words and symbols from one of the sheets. Glue an envelope on the back of the laminated worksheet for the symbols/words that have been cut apart.

Worksheet —Vocabulary Review

As a vocabulary review use the worksheet on page 252. Students fill in the sentences using the symbols/words at the top of the page. This page can be used as a worksheet or a discussion page. It also makes a good homework page.

Magazines: Big On Bottom, Small On Top

In almost all office or public area cleaning, there are stacks of paper and/or magazines that need to be straightened. The concept that the larger magazines (or papers) should go on the bottom of the stack and the smaller ones on top is often difficult.

Skill: *Stacking magazines and papers.*

Activity: Teach this skill with only two magazines that are very different in size. Show students what can happen if you stack the large ones on top of the small ones (they will slide off or fall to the floor). This small on top concept was touched on in the **Retail Unit** concerning boxes. The concept is the same. Once the concept is introduced, give ample practice. Spread several magazines out on a table and assign a student to stack them all up in one pile. You can vary the number of magazines and the difference in size based on the skill level of the students. The concepts of big and small are important here.

Media Center Volunteers

The school media center is the logical place to let students practice the straightening skills. Most media centers have an area where magazines are left out on the tables. Students could straighten these up. Talk to the media center personnel, they may have other ideas that your students can participate in for this skill.

Dust And Wipe

All jobs require some type of cleaning and/or wiping of flat surfaces. Begin by letting students clean off bookshelves in your classroom. Then branch out to other areas of the school.

Pick It Up

Teach students that it is everyone's job to keep trash off the floor. Start by going in small groups around the building or school grounds and picking up trash. Parking lots and athletic fields are a prime source of practice in this skill. It is a very important habit for students to develop. An employee who stops and picks up trash in the workplace is more likely to keep his/her job than one who steps over it because *" I didn't put it there!"* This is one of those small things that makes employees valuable and likeable.

First Impressions Are Important

The maintenance crew in most schools are kept very busy. Talk with administration about setting up a cleaning schedule for the public areas in your school. This is a perfect situation for more realistic practice in general cleaning skills: dusting, emptying trash, straightening magazines and papers, or even sweeping. Some offices have windows and glass doors that can never be kept clean. Set up a schedule and let students take turns on this assignment. Develop a picture checklist like the one described in the next activity to make students as independent as possible.

I Just Can't Remember

Remember that independent work is the goal of any work training program. Here are several ways to help students reach this goal in general cleaning tasks.

- Use a flip chart like the one on pages 249 and 250.

- Use a picture checklist. This technique is used often in areas where the workers may not speak English. See the **Picture Checklist For Cleaning,** page 253, for an example.

- A wallet-sized photo album can be used like a flip chart with either photos or line drawings.

- See **Flip That Chart**, page 245, for a description of how to use Velcro and cardboard to make a sequencing strip.

- For students who can read, a written list that allows the student to check off the steps as they are done can be very helpful in keeping the students on task. See the **Written Checklist for Cleaning,** page 254, as an example.

- Another technique is to use a personal stereo headset for the student. Record the instructions in order. The student plays the tape to hear the first step. He then turns off the tape until the task is complete. The tape is turned back on to hear the second step. For students who can follow verbal directions, this is an easy way to increase their independence and keep them on task.

Flip Chart 1
Emptying the Trash

Steps to Empty Trash

1. Is it full?

2. Tie bag.

3. Lift out carefully.

4. Reline can.

5. Dispose of bag.

Worksheet
Vocabulary Practice

Name _____ Date _____

Directions: Match the words to the correct symbol, then write the word.

empty	**empty**	
trash	**trash**	
bag	**bag**	
tie	**tie**	
careful	**careful**	
work	**work**	
clean	**clean**	
housekeeping	**housekeeping**	

Worksheet
Vocabulary Review

Name_____ **Date**_____

Directions: Use the words/symbols at the top of the page to fill in the correct word in each sentence below.

trash can	lift	full	empty	tied

1. Before you empty a trash can, check to see if it is _____ .

2. The place where people in an office put their trash is called a _____ .

3. If a trash can is full, you need to _____ it.

4. After the bag is tied, you _____ it out.

5. Trash bags should be _____ so the trash does not fall out.

Picture Checklist For Cleaning

Empty trash.

Put liner in trash can.

Take items off table.

Dust table.

Put items back on table.

Dust lamp shade.

Sweep floor.

Straighten furniture.

Turn off lights.

Written Checklist For Cleaning

- [ ] 1. Empty trash can.

- [ ] 2. Put liner in trash can.

- [ ] 3. Take all items off table.

- [ ] 4. Dust the table.

- [ ] 5. Put items back on the table.

- [ ] 6. Dust lamp shade.

- [ ] 7. Sweep floor.

- [ ] 8. Straighten up furniture.

- [ ] 9. Turn off the lights.

Bedroom Cleaning Skills

> ## Laundry/Housekeeping: Objective 4B
>
> *Skills needed to clean a bedroom.*

Suggested Activities

Name That Sheet
Before students can be independent working at a housekeeping job, they need to learn to identify types of bedding or at least match to sample. Collect several examples of the following:

sheets (flat & fitted)	blankets	pillows
bedspreads	pillowcase	

Use the **Bedding Identification Overlay,** page 259, for identification or yes/no responses while learning to identify bedding. At this point, introduce the name, symbol, and use of each item. The **Bedding Labeling Activity Sheet**, page 260, has the words and symbols. Copy the page and laminate for labeling use.

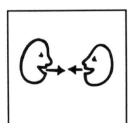

Vocabulary, Vocabulary, Vocabulary
The following words are vocabulary words for this objective:

flat sheet	fitted sheet	pillow
pillowcase	blanket	bedspread

Review these words with your students and use the following activities to reinforce the words.

Worksheet — Vocabulary Practice
The **Vocabulary Practice Worksheet,** page 261, is designed to allow practice in writing while reviewing work-related words.

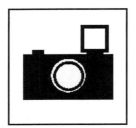

A Photo Is Worth A Thousand Words

Skill: *Recognizing photos of real bedding items.*
Activity: Take photos of real beds and bedding. Make double prints and use them as a matching game. If possible, get "one-use cameras" and let the students take pictures at home (remember to get cameras with a flash). Students can take pictures of their beds and bedding. The words from the **Bedding Identification Overlay,** page 259, can be used to match with these photos for additional vocabulary practice.

Posters

Use ads from retail stores and linen stores to make posters.

Skill: *Recognizing bedding vocabulary words.*
Activity: Have students cut out the pictures in the ads to make posters. Make a poster for each of the words or let individuals make posters with all the words on them.

Match Game

Copy the **Bedding Labeling Activity Sheet,** page 260, four or more times onto colored paper. Laminate and cut apart. Students can use these to play match games at various levels:

Skill: *Recognizing and matching bedding vocabulary words.*
Game 1: Matching. Place one of each word face up on the table. Have students turn over one other card and match to correct word. This can be made simpler by having three blank cards and only one card with a word on it. Then the student must match the word card to the word card.
Game 2: Concentration-Matching. All the cards are shuffled and turned face down. Students take turns choosing two cards, if the cards match, they may keep them. If they do not match, they are turned back over and the next student takes a turn.

Seeing Double

Skill: *Sorting vocabulary pictures.*
Activity: Contact linen stores for sales circulars. Cut out matching pictures and mount on 4x6 cards, then laminate. Make multiple cards by using the same picture from several ads. These cards can then be used as a sorting activity. Glue one of the pictures (use the word cards for literacy/vocabulary practice) to a large envelope (laminate the envelope first for increased durability). Students can then sort the ad cards into the correct envelope.

Worksheet — Making Up The Bed
Use the **Making Up The Bed Worksheet,** page 262, to help students think about the items to make up a bed. This can be done as an independent activity or as a great discussion starter activity.

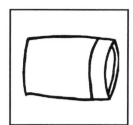

Pillows In The Pillowcases

Skill: *Putting pillows in pillowcases.*
Activity: Demonstrate putting a pillowcase on a pillow. Begin with pillows that are much smaller than the pillow case. Let students practice putting on pillowcases. Students who are not physically able to do this can be paired with other students to give directions or do quality checks. This is a difficult task for most students and may require a great deal of practice. Increase the size of the pillows until the students can put a standard pillow into a standard pillowcase.

Relay Race
Put a little fun into the practice of putting on pillowcases by having a relay race.

Skill: *Practice putting pillowcases onto pillows.*
Activity: Divide the group into teams. Have one pillow and pillowcase for each student participating. Place the pillows and cases at one end of the area and line the teams up single file at the other end (a hallway works well for this). On signal, one person from each team runs to the other end and puts a pillow in the pillowcase and brings it back to the next teammate in line. That person puts the pillow down and runs to get another pillow and puts it in a pillowcase and brings it back to the next team mate. This continues until all the pillows are cased. The winning team is the one that finishes first. Be sure to include students who aren't able to physically compete by setting up overlays for them to be cheerleaders on their team. Use the **Race Overlay,** page 263. It will be much more fun if you personalize the overlay to include names of students and/or teams.

Bed Making
This is an essential skill in many housekeeping jobs. It is also a skill that is almost impossible to practice without a real bed, which creates a problem in most classrooms. This time you may have to get very creative. Some possibilities include a small cot, an air mattress, a crib-size mattress, cardboard boxes duct taped together to form a bed. Of course a real bed is the best. The following activities assume that you have access to a bed or a reasonable facsimile.

Stripping A Bed

Students who are unable to make a bed may be able to strip a bed and be paired with other workers. In one hotel situation, an intellectually impaired student was paired with other housekeeping workers. Her main job was to strip the dirty beds and empty the trash cans. She also retrieved items from the housekeeping storage area as needed by the other workers so they could keep working without having to stop and get materials. Students should be taught the following steps for stripping a bed:

1. Remove the bedspread and place on a chair or floor.
2. Remove the blanket and place on top of the bedspread.
3. Take the pillowcases off an put in the middle of the bed; put the pillows on the bedspread.
4. Pull up each corner and toss to the middle of the bed so that after all four corners are up, the dirty sheets are in the middle of the bed.
5. Carefully gather up the dirty sheets and carry to the laundry hamper. Be sure to stress not putting their faces into the dirty sheets which seems to be a natural response for many students.

On The Road Again

Contact local hotels for a demonstration of their housekeeping jobs. Many hotels have a standard that the entire room be cleaned within 20 minutes. Needless to say, their cleaning procedures and standards are much different than most people use at home. If possible, visit several different hotels/motels to see the different ways that they are trained. Also ask if there is a manual which states their standards. Don't forget to check and see if they have any training videos you can borrow.

Bedding IdentificationOverlay

flat sheet
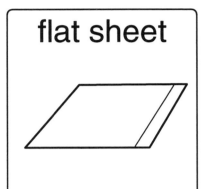

blanket

fitted sheet

pillow

pillowcase

bedspread

Bedding Labeling Activity

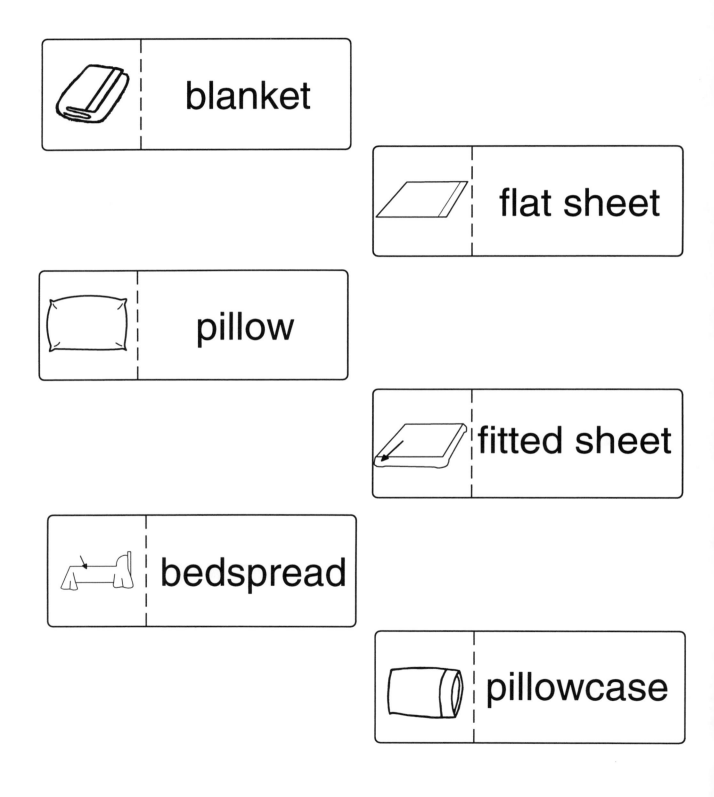

blanket

flat sheet

pillow

fitted sheet

bedspread

pillowcase

Worksheet
Vocabulary Practice

Name _____ Date _____

Directions: Write the vocabulary words below. They are all words about things you would use to make a bed.

	flat sheet	
	fitted sheet	
	pillow	
	pillowcase	
	blanket	
	bedspread	

Worksheet
Making Up The Bed

Name _____ Date _____

Directions: Circle the pictures of things you would use to make up a bed.
Put an "X" on things you would not need to make up a bed.

---

flat sheet
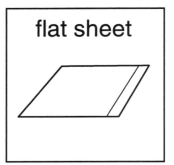

paint

shirt

bedspread
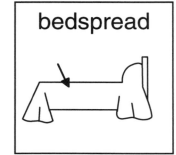

blanket

pillow
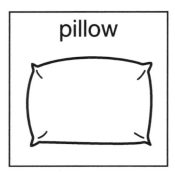

beach umbrella

pillowcase
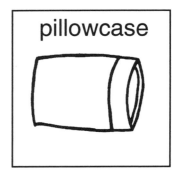

can opener

fitted sheet

Race Overlay

ready	wait a minute **1**	go
winner	finish	good sport **2**
fast	slow	I win

Bathroom Cleaning Skills

Laundry/Housekeeping: Objective 4C
Skills needed to clean a bathroom.

Everyone cringes at this skill—teachers, parents, and usually students. However, it is a necessary skill for a housekeeping job and a *really* helpful skill for independent (or even family) living. Latex gloves can be used or the heavier gloves used for dishwashing. While this is not a "fun" job, it really needs to be taught and practiced.

Suggested Activities

How Well Do You Know Your Bathroom?
The first step in any job is to be sure you know the vocabulary. In this case, that also means knowing what is supposed to be in the bathroom.

Skill: *Recognizing bathroom vocabulary words.*
Activity: Use the **Bathroom Vocabulary Activities 1 & 2,** pages 269 & 270, to help identify items in the bathroom. Activity 1 uses symbols and Activity 2 uses words. Of course, a real bathroom is much better and makes things more concrete. Perhaps take your students on a bathroom "tour" and use the activity sheet. Use either the **Bathroom Vocabulary Overlay 1 or 2,** pages 271-272, for this activity.

toilet	sink	tub
counter	floor	shower
mirror	faucet	drain

Worksheet—Where Do I Go?
In the **Where Do I Go Worksheet,** page 273, students are given a chance to identify the items discussed in the above activity. They are asked to draw a line from the bathroom item to the correct place in the bathroom. Use **Bathroom Vocabulary Overlay 1 or 2,** pages 271-272, with this activity.

Worksheet — General Cleaning Vocabulary Practice
In this additional vocabulary worksheet on page 274, students are asked to fill in the blank with the correct word and/or symbol. Use **Bathroom Vocabulary Overlay 1 or 2,** pages 271-272, with this activity.

Ready, Set, Brush

Since cleaning an actual toilet is not only a distasteful task, but not an easy one to do in a classroom, here is a little activity to at least practice the basic skills. The **Clean/Dirty Overlay,** page 275 works well with this activity.

Skill: *Recognizing bathroom vocabulary words.*
Activity: You will need a large bucket (the kind that restaurants use for pudding and yogurt mixes will work nicely), a toilet brush, and lots of water. Fill the bucket and use the toilet brush to demonstrate cleaning a toilet. Have the students pretend that the bucket is a toilet and practice cleaning. Use gloves here to help the students learn to work using gloves. If at all possible, progress to a real toilet. Talk to the maintenance staff about safety and health procedures. It is a job that many people do, no matter how "yucky."

Clean That Sink

Sinks and bathtubs are often the dirtiest items in a bathroom. A bathtub is really just a large sink sitting on the floor. If students can clean a sink, they can easily progress to cleaning a tub. This is helpful since sinks are readily available at school, but bathtubs are not.

Skill: *Using the correct method to clean a sink and bathtub.*
Activity: Use spray cleaners, not powders. It may help to add food coloring to clear cleaners to help the students become aware of the entire surface. Other things that the student needs to become aware of are:

- The drain should be cleaned of any hair, trash, etc.
- The faucets should be wiped dry after cleaning.
- The sink (or tub) should be wiped dry after cleaning.

This is another one of those skills that needs lots of practice. Check with your home economics lab or even the science labs to see if you can practice cleaning their sinks. The **Cleaning Sinks & Toilets Overlay,** Page 276, will be of assistance with this activity and ones that will follow.

Worksheet — Picture/Word Matching

Using the **Picture/Word Matching Worksheet**, page 277, Cut out pictures from catalogs, magazines, and newspaper ads to go with the words. Possible adaptations for this activity include:

- The teacher can cut out the pictures ahead of time and read the words so students can identify the correct picture.

- Precut pictures, tape in correct place, copy, and laminate. Then let students match precut pictures to the laminated sheets.

- Copy the worksheet; cut the worksheet into three sections and enlarge. Students can either match or answer yes/no when asked if it is a correct match. The **Bathroom Vocabulary Overlay 2**, page 272, can also be used for this activity.

Don't Forget The Experts!

No matter how much of a cleaning expert you consider yourself to be, you are probably in for an education when it comes to quick cleaning in the real world. No one cleans at work like they do at home. Talk to and visit as many sites as you can with the class. People and places to check into are:

- Hotel housekeeping departments
- Hotel training videos
- Technical School programs with hotel and restaurant management programs

Straight From the Horse's Mouth

It may be easier to get speakers to come to your class and talk than to get your students to several sites for tours. Be sure to explain specifically to the people you've invited what you want them to share with your students and why. If not, they will assume you want a more "academic" type speech. What you are looking for are people who can talk to your students about what types of jobs there are, what kind of work they have to be able to do, and other relevant details like how much money do they make and how easy/hard is it to get a job in this field in your area. Some people to keep in mind:

- Professional cleaning services
- Mini-Maid type housecleaning services
- Human resources people to talk about jobs in the industry
- Vocational rehabilitation personnel to talk about job placement and training

Worksheet — More Vocabulary Practice
The **More Vocabulary Practice Worksheet,** page 278, is a review of some of the words used in the laundry/housekeeping environment. Students are asked to write/copy the words. Students who have reading skills could write sentences with the words. The **Bathroom Vocabulary Overlay 2,** page 272, works well here.

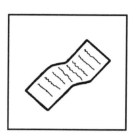

Check It Off

The checklist concept works very well for cleaning the bathroom. The **Written Checklist for Cleaning,** page 279, is an example of a picture checklist for cleaning the bathroom. If the checklist is laminated, crayon or wax pens can be used to check off the tasks and then the checklist can be used again. Or it can be copied and the completed checklist turned into the teacher/supervisor for data collection. Most students like the independence of using a checklist. Pictures can be used in place of words (see the **Picture Checklist for Cleaning,** page 280).

Picture This!

If the checklist is too abstract for students, take a photo of each step and put them in a flip type photo album so that students can flip the page after each task.

Worksheet — Cleaning Bathroom Review
This worksheet, page 281, offers the opportunity for students to answer work-related questions with a yes/no response. Don't forget to use augmentative devices. Any overlay with a yes/no response can be used for most of these activities. Overlays on pages 271-272 & 275-276 are especially useful.

Worksheet
Picture Bathroom Vocabulary Activity 1

Name _____ Date _____

Directions: Draw a line from the bathroom item to the correct place in the bathroom.

shower

counter

bathtub

mirror

sink

faucet

toilet

floor

drain

Worksheet
Bathroom Vocabulary Activity 2

Name _____ Date _____

Directions: Draw a line from the bathroom word to the correct place in the bathroom.

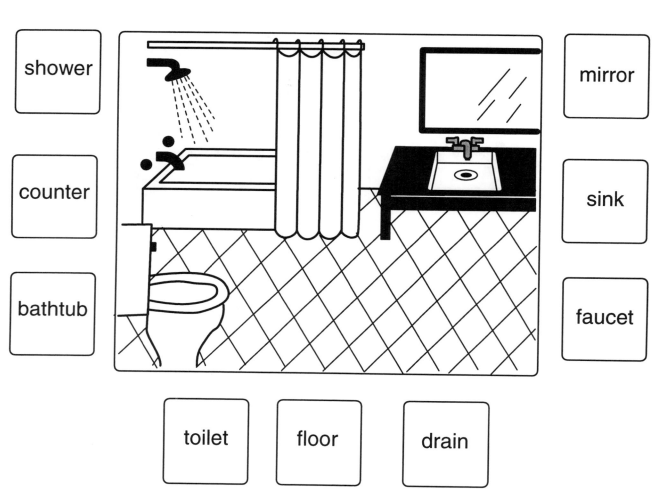

shower

counter

bathtub

mirror

sink

faucet

toilet

floor

drain

Bathroom Vocabulary Overlay 1

mirror

counter

sink

faucet

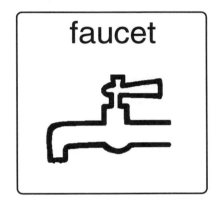

yes

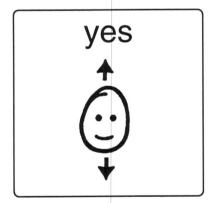

no

Bathroom Vocabulary Overlay 2

toilet

floor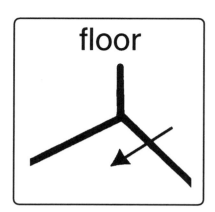

bathtub

mirror

counter

shower

sink

faucet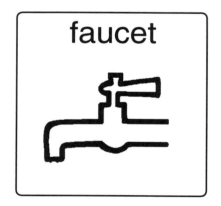

drain

yes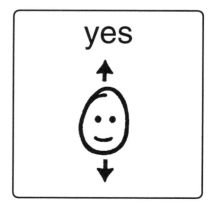

no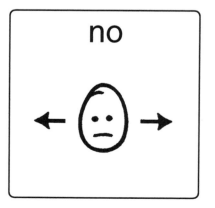

Worksheet
Where Do I Go?

Name _____ Date _____

Directions: Draw a line from the words/pictures to the correct place for that item in the bathroom.

shower

counter

bathtub

mirror

sink

faucet

toilet

floor

drain

Worksheet
General Cleaning Vocabulary Practice

Name _____ Date _____

Directions: Fill in the blanks in the sentences below with the correct word/symbol.

floor	carpet	dust	vacuum	counter

1. To clean surfaces, you will need to [   ] them.

2. The space beside the sink is the [   ].

3. To clean the [   ] you will need a mop.

4. If you [   ] the floor walking backwards, you will cover your footprints.

5. To clean the carpet, you will need a [   ].

Teacher Directions: Make extra copies of the word blocks for students who cannot write and let them match the blocks to the question on the worksheet. Students who have the ability may write sentences or dictate sentences to each other.

Clean/Dirty Overlay

toilet

clean

dirty

yes

no

Cleaning Sinks & Toilets Overlay

toilet

sink

clean

dirty

yes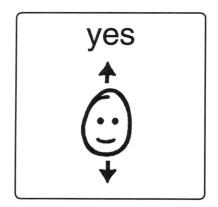

no

Worksheet
Picture/Word Matching

Name _____ Date _____

Directions: Cut out pictures and glue them to these vocabulary words.

toilet	sink	bathtub
mirror	towel	counter
door	mat	towel rack

Worksheet
More Vocabulary Practice

Name _____ Date _____

Directions: Write the vocabulary words below. They are all words about things you would use to clean in a house or hotel.

	toilet	
	toilet	

	sink	
	sink	

	bathtub	
	bathtub	

	mirror	
	mirror	

	shower	
	shower	

Written Checklist For Cleaning

☐ 1. Take out dirty towels.

☐ 2. Pick up trash.

☐ 3. Clean sink.

☐ 4. Dust table.

☐ 5. Clean mirror.

☐ 6. Clean toilet.

☐ 7. Clean floor.

☐ 8. Put in clean supplies.

☐ 9. Turn off lights.

Laundry / Housekeeping Unit

Picture Checklist for Cleaning

Take out dirty towels.

Pick up trash.

Clean sink.

Clean tub.

Clean mirror.

Clean toilet.

Clean floor.

Put in clean supplies.

Turn off lights.

Worksheet
Cleaning Bathroom Review

Name_____ Date_____

Directions: Read the sentences and pick [yes] or [no] .

1. When you clean a mirror, start from the top and go to the bottom. [yes] [no]

2. When you clean a sink, don't worry about the faucets, they don't need cleaning. [yes] [no]

3. When cleaning a toilet, it's a good idea to use a toilet brush. [yes] [no]

4. It's a good idea to clean the floor first, and then the rest of the bathroom. [yes] [no]

5. When you clean a bathroom, don't bother to hang up clean towels—someone else may do it. [yes] [no]

6. The tub never gets dirty—don't waste your time cleaning it. [yes] [no]

7. When you clean the bathroom, be sure to wipe off the counters. [yes] [no]

8. A dirty bathroom can be unhealthy. [yes] [no]

Laundry / Housekeeping Unit

General Room Cleaning Skills

The skills from the previous sections (cleaning open areas, making a bed, and cleaning a bathroom) go together to provide the skills to clean a room in a hotel situation or even in a hospital. These activities and materials are provided to help you integrate these skills for your students. They are only suggestions and will have to be adapted to your situation and student needs.

Suggested Activities

Picture Checklist
For nonreading students, this is the most efficient way to give them the tasks needed and allow for independence. This method is used in many housekeeping jobs for non-English speaking employees. See the sample **Picture Checklist For Cleaning,** page 285, as an example of a picture checklist that was actually used by a student at a work training site. It is also helpful if you have several students working on the same room. They can mark off the tasks they have done and not redo a job someone else has finished already.

Write It Down!
For students who can read, a written checklist works well. See the **Checklist For Cleaning Hotel Rooms,** page 286, for an example of a written list that was used by a student at a work training site. It is important to be specific and use simple language. This can be combined with the **Picture Checklist For Cleaning,** page 285.

Role Play

The **Following A Checklist Role Play,** pages 287-289, gives students a chance to practice communication skills as well as use problem-solving skills. Use the overlay provided, page 290, for full participation.

Worksheet—Cleaning Method Matchup

In this worksheet, page 291, students are asked to match the situation with the correct cleaning method. This is an excellent discussion page for small group activity.

Worksheet—Correct Cleaning Order

Students are asked to put cleaning activities in sequential order. It may be necessary to actually attempt the illustrated activities to allow the students to experience the sequence of activities (see page292). Laminate the worksheet and cut apart so that students can actually put pictures in order. Try the idea for Velcro sequencing described on page 245, **Flip That Chart.**

What's Your Idea?

Included are three pages of general picture symbols, pages 293-29, for cleaning activities and tasks so that you can cut and paste your own picture checklist.

Picture Checklist For Cleaning
(Fellowship Hall)

☐	**1. Wash/dust paneling and doors in hallway.**	
☐	**2. Stack chairs.**	
☐	**3. Vacuum classrooms.**	
☐	**4. Wash tables.**	
☐	**5. Empty trashcans.**	
☐	**6. Straighten nursery.**	
☐	**7. Replace chairs around tables.**	
☐	**8. Take trash bags to dumpster.**	Dumpster

Checklist For Cleaning Hotel Rooms

☐ 1. Strip dirty laundry
- — sheets
- — pillowcases
- — towels/washcloths
- — drop dirty linen into chute

☐ 2. Trash
- — pick up trash around room
- — throw away opened soap
- — empty trash
- — reline trash can

☐ 3. Clean sink and counter

☐ 4. Clean tub
- — scrub tub
- — wipe walls
- — rinse well
- — place bathmat over side of tub

☐ 5. Clean toilet
- — scrub toilet with brush
- — wipe off exterior part of toilet
- — flush

☐ 6. Clean mirrors

☐ 7. Counter top
- — place 3 clean glasses on counter
- — put ice bucket to left of sink
- — place extra toilet tissue on back of toilet

☐ 8. Linens
- — put 4 towels out
- — put 4 washclothes out

☐ 9. Make bed

☐ 10. Vacuum

☐ 11. Turn off lights

Role Play: Following a Checklist

Jessie and Donny are working at a large hotel. Their job is to clean rooms for the guests. The hotel provides a checklist for them so they will know exactly what to do, but Jessie seems to have some trouble following it. Read this role play to see what happens:

Jessie: Donny, let's turn on the television while we clean this room. My favorite show is about to come on.

Donny: No, Jessie, you know that's against the rules. Mrs. Dillard said we aren't supposed to watch TV while we are working.

Jessie: Come on, Donny, nobody will know. She almost never comes to check on us anymore.

Donny: That's because she has been out of town. She got back yesterday, and besides, she trusts us. I don't want to mess this up.

Jessie: Oh, Donny, you're such a wimp.

Donny: Jessie, what are you doing now?

Jessie: What does it look like? I am about to run the vacuum cleaner.

Donny: But the checklist says that we are supposed to make the beds, then dust and clean the bathroom. Vacuuming is the last thing on our list.

Jessie: So what? Who cares about that stupid old checklist anyway? I don't think it's really any big deal if we do things out of order. There are just too many rules around here. It's getting on my nerves.

Mrs. Dillard: Hello Donny, Jessie. How is everything going in here?

Jessie (*surprised*): Oh, hi, Mrs. Dillard.

Mrs. Dillard: Jessie, are you already vacuuming? Have you finished the other parts of the checklist?

Jessie: Um... no, I just thought I would get the vacuuming out of the way. It doesn't really matter, does it?

Mrs. Dillard: Yes, Jessie, it does matter. When you vacuum first, then you have two problems. First, you wipe the dust onto the clean floor, and second, you walk all over your freshly vacuumed carpet, and get footprints all over it. If you vacuum last, you can walk out backwards and vacuum over your footprints. That way, the room looks nice and clean for the guests.

Jessie: I see. I'm sorry, Mrs. Dillard. From now on I'll follow the checklist.

Donny: Mrs. Dillard, I have a question. I don't know what to do. On my checklist it says I am supposed to put out soap with a blue wrapper in the shower and soap with a green wrapper by the sink. We don't have any more green soap.

Mrs. Dillard: Donny, I'm glad you told me. For today, put soap with a blue wrapper in both places. I'll go order some more green soap right away. By the way, I'm glad to see that the TV is not on. I just had to get after one of the other workers about that. When guests walk by and see our staff watching TV, it may make them think we are not very good workers. Keep up the good work, you two. I'll see you in a little while!

Jessie: Wow, Donny, you were right. We really do need to follow the checklist. I will from now on.

Questions:

Read the Checklist Role Play to answer the questions:

1. Why did Donny tell Jessie not to turn on the TV?
    a. It is against the rules.
    b. Donny does not like to watch TV.
    c. The TV was broken.

2. Who is Mrs. Dillard?
    a. A guest
    b. The boss
    c. Donny's mother

3. Why did Mrs. Dillard tell Jessie she should save the vacuuming until last?
    a. She just liked it better that way.
    b. If she vacuumed first, she would wipe dust onto the clean carpet and put footprints all over the carpet.
    c. Mrs. Dillard's mother had taught her to do that.

4. Do you think Jessie will follow the checklist next time? Why or why not?

5. Mrs. Dillard is going to give a promotion to either Donny or Jessie next week. Which one do you think she will pick. Why?

Role Play Overlay

a	**b**	**c**
yes	I don't know.	no
Donny	Mrs. Dillard	Jessie

Worksheet
Cleaning Method Matchup

Name _____ Date _____

Directions: Match each situation below with the correct cleaning method.

_____

carpet
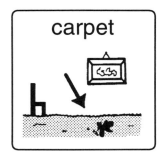

wipe
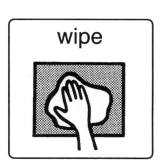

counter

mop

floor

vacuum

window
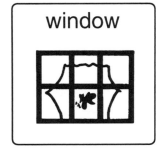

glass cleaner

Worksheet
Correct Cleaning Order

Name _____ Date _____

Directions: What is the best order to do these jobs? Think of working from top to bottom. Then put the numbers 1, 2, or 3 in the correct boxes.

wash windows	☐	plug in vacuum	☐
mop floor	☐	vacuum floor	☐
wipe counter	☐	dust furniture	☐

Sample Symbols 1

toilet paper 	pass out cups 	soap 	matches 
book 	sweep 	sweep 	fold 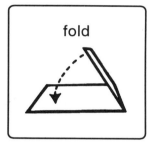
telephone 	broom 	push broom 	menu 
towel 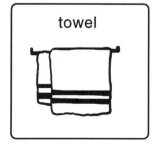	washcloth 	mat 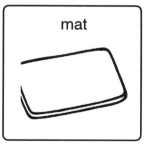	laundromat 
pass out placemats 	pencil 	vacuum cleaner 	knock 

Sample Symbols 2

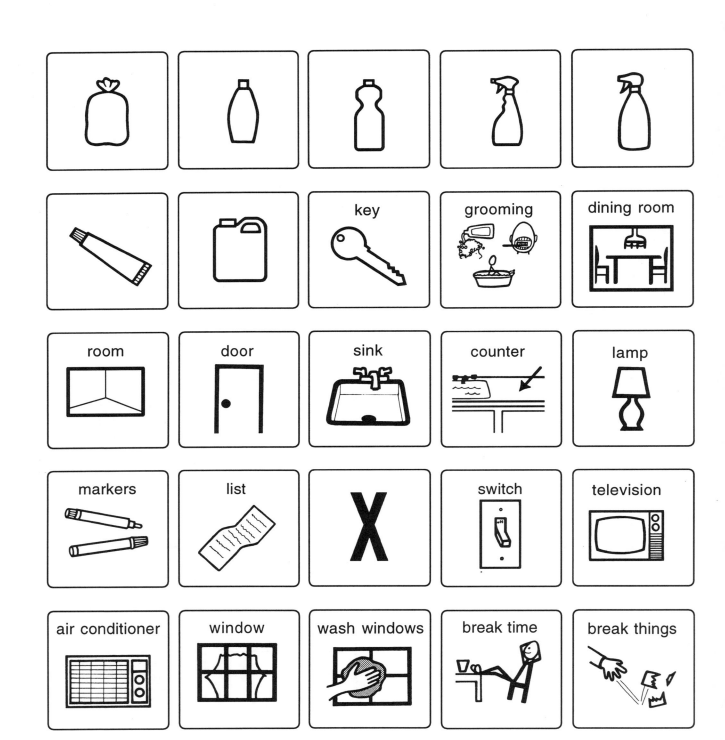

		key	grooming	dining room
room	door	sink	counter	lamp
markers	list	X	switch	television
air conditioner	window	wash windows	break time	break things

Sample Symbols 3

bed 	bedroom 	make bed 	make bed 	pillow 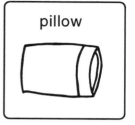
sheets 	blanket 	dresser 	desk 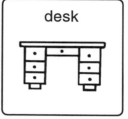	table 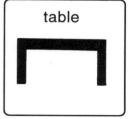
wipe table 	chair 	mirror 	clean 	dirty 
cleaner 	cleaning 	clean room 	bathroom 	bathtub 
cleanser 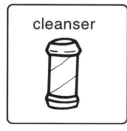	clean 	clean 	shower 	toilet 

Laundry / Housekeeping Unit